My Sister the Father

By: Meri Whitaker

TABLE OF CONTENTS

FOREWORD

The church of Jesus Christ is at its best when it forthrightly and respectfully embraces the poor. The poor have a unique way of connecting our lives with Jesus and with God's work in the world. Ministry with the poor consistently "preaches the Gospel to us", offering deliverance from petty obsessions and the captivity of possessions.

Amidst the spate of books telling us how to do ministry, it is refreshing to encounter an uncomplicated, clear witness to Christian ministry effectively and humbly lived.

Meri Whitaker knows the Gospel and "does" the Gospel in a fashion that reflects solid theology, pastoral care, and respectful servant hood. Her setting for ministry reflects the holistic nature of proclamation and service. John Wesley would be pleased with the way in which she embodies "holiness of heart and holiness of life".

The author has given us a book that will enrich our daily walk with God. Many of us will use this book for daily devotional reading. The book provides a manual for missionary service, guiding the reader in a ministry style of sensitivity, respect, patience, trust and holy confidence. Beyond that is the inspiring testimony to the ways in which God's presence and power inform, enliven, and transform the lives of pastor, missionaries, congregations, and of course, God's cherished "poor children".

In poignant stories Meri Whitaker has given " a face" to the marginalized and has troubled "the place" of so many of us who become secure in possessions and positions. Her stories embody "the Story" of God's grace and mission in such a fashion as to be an oasis for parched spirits and a guide for aspiring servants. As one reads her book, it becomes clear that each of us has a great need and a great gift, but none of us is above another. We are all alike at the feet of Jesus, the "Master who acts as a slave to them".

When one concludes reading this volume, one is left with the haunting admonition, "go thou and do likewise".

Dan E. Solomon
Bishop In Residence
McMurry University
Abilene, Texas
(formerly Meri's bishop)

INTRODUCTION

Where Did that Title Come From?

I was raised in a home that had very little knowledge of the workings of people in the ministry. I have five sisters and one brother. The first Easter that I was in the ministry, I was serving a large church in up-state New York. I lived in a huge parsonage and I wanted my family to come and experience what I did for a living.

They all arrived with their families...several of my sisters had married Catholic boys. They sat in some of the front pews and took up two full rows.

It was "High" church. We processed in with full regalia; robes and stoles. The choir sang, the lilies were draped over the altar in the shape of a cross. It was an impressive service.

I went home for lunch expecting the rave reviews from my family. I was sitting in a dining room chair when my four year old niece came in and put her arm up on my knee and said, "Aunt Meri, I didn't know you were an altar boy." Her mother gasped and escorted her from the room where she was overheard saying, "Aunt Meri is NOT an altar boy...Aunt Meri is a FATHER!"

My ministry has essentially been in four locations. I began ministry in Anadarko, Oklahoma serving as a seminary intern with several tribes in Western OK. After seminary I went to Lockport, New York as the Director of Christian Education and Minister of Missions. When I left there I took the position as the Director of Campus Ministry at Bacone College, a small college aimed at Native American Students. From there I went to Cookson, Oklahoma, a tiny little town on Lake Tenkiller and that is where most of my ministry has been. I have had two stories published in the Upper Room.

THANKS

My thanks go to the many who have been a part of my life and given me these stories through our times together. I want to mention my God who has placed me in an awesome ministry and allowed me to see His great works every day that I have served there. I also want to thank my brother, Bill Whitaker who spent countless hours reading and fixing this book so that it was presentable. I want to thank the United Methodist Church for the honor of serving as their missionary, Debbie Humphrey for seeing my vision for the cover of the book, Boyce Bowdon and Bishop Dan Solomon for pushing me to write down my experiences and I want to thank my family and my church for all of their support.

CHAPTER ONE

"You are My witnesses" declares the Lord,
"And My servant whom I've chosen…"
ISAIAH 43:10

IN HIS TIME!

"To everything there is a season and a time to every purpose under the heaven...I know that whatsoever God does, it will be forever; nothing will be taken from it or added to it. God does it."
Ecclesiastes 3:1 & 14

There are so many times in ministry when "I" have an idea and "I" take off with it and when it fails, then "I" am confused about why God didn't bless my efforts. And yet, when I spend time in prayer asking God to give me direction and to open doors before I begin with anything new, I am always awe struck as I watch doors fly open and resources become available.

MY "CALL"

I was a late bloomer by most people's definition. I waited until April to decide that I wanted to go to college in the fall. I attended college for one reason and one reason only; to play ball. I was pretty good and playing volleyball was the entire focus of my life. I truly believed that my talent as a player would carry me directly into a wonderful teaching job as a coach. Imagine my surprise when I found out that it meant very little to the administrators who would employee me.

I spent the next four years coaching, officiating, teaching in country schools in Upstate New York, and immersing myself in volunteer ministry at the First Baptist Church of Rome, New York. People in the church began to see the potential for professional ministry in me, and they encouraged and supported me in a decision to go to seminary.

I decided to attend Gordon Conwell Theological Seminary in South Hamilton, Massachusetts. The seminary was ten minutes from the ocean, ten minutes from Salem, and twenty minutes by train to Boston.

As I packed my light green Pinto and headed east on the New York State Thruway I found myself praying a prayer that went something like this:

"Lord, I have given up everything to follow you. I quit my job, I left my home, I left my friends and I left the church. I would go anywhere to serve you, I would do anything to serve you. Just don't ask me to go into the inner city and don't ask me to go on the mission field."

Six weeks later I was walking the streets of Boston involved in a street ministry as the result of a class I was taking in seminary and within the year I was serving as a mission intern in Anadarko, Oklahoma.

I guess the message was not that I served a God that "made" me do the things that I didn't want to do. It was not that I needed to learn to trust God even in the things that would be difficult for me, as so many scholars tried to persuade me to believe. The message for me was that I served a God that knew me better than I knew myself. This God knew that the mission field was the place that I could serve for a lifetime and be perfectly happy and totally fulfilled.

MEMORIES OF SEMINARY

Seminary was a highlight in my life and it was, without a doubt, a time of learning to trust God in all of my decisions. I was as poor as a person can be while at Gordon Conwell, all the while living in one of the more affluent towns in Massachusetts. The money in South Hamilton was old money and the town sported one of the only hunt and polo clubs left in existence.

I found a job at a local pharmacy and spent the evenings dusting shelves, pricing items and checking out customers. I would tell people that I earned my way through seminary "selling drugs." It didn't take long for me to realize that my little paycheck was very limiting and so I had to make some rather difficult decisions. I discovered that the school cafeteria offered the condiments for lunch free of charge and peanut butter was a condiment. I began bringing an apple for lunch, dishing up some peanut butter to spread on it and drinking water. My lunch averaged out to $.05/day. I walked everywhere I needed to go in town and my social life was confined to fellowship with other students at my house.

One night, a friend of mine came over for a visit when I was on my way to a workshop for the weekend. I invited her to go along and when we got back she got into her car and attempted to start it. It would not turn over. It was late, so I told her stay the night and we would try to get it started in the morning. The next morning was cold, well below zero, and try as we might, even a jump would not start the stubborn car. I was getting frustrated because I wanted to be at the next session of the workshop, so once again I invited her to come along.

That night we tried again to start the car and it would not even groan. She was invited and stayed a second night at my house and on Sunday morning we headed down again to try to start the car. No luck! We went to church and then on to the conclusion of the workshop. After we got home and had eaten dinner, my friend announced that she was going to go and start her car. She said that she was convinced that God had wanted her to go to the workshop and that the car would start now.

I believed in God and I believed in miracles but I did not believe that the car was going to start. Car batteries do not lose their charge in sub-zero temperatures for days and then suddenly get charged up again. I told my friend this and prepared her for another night's stay at my house but she was determined that the car would start. I followed her down to the driveway and watched as she climbed into the car.

"It won't start" I insisted. She put the key in the ignition, turned it over once and it started without the slightest hesitation. She smiled a satisfied smile and backed out leaving me to wonder at the power of God.

ANADARKO

The summer between my first and second year in seminary, I was required to have an internship in my field of study. I had made the decision to go on the mission field, so I contacted my Pastor and asked him to help me find a place. He recommended a place in western Oklahoma called Anadarko. The American Baptist Churches had mission work there and it seemed to be a good place to start. I accepted an opportunity to work at the Community Center with Vacation Bible Schools, recreation, and the youth.

I left New York State in May of 1979 with no idea where I was going or what I was to do. It was 59° in NY when I got on the plane. It was 100° in Oklahoma when I got off the plane. I was picked up by one of the missionaries that I would be working with and we visited on the hour-long trip home from the airport. I would be staying at the Wichita Mission. It was out of town, but there was a parsonage where I would be living. When we arrived at the mission I noticed a small area with a fence around it and a cross in the center. I was curious about it but I decided to wait and see if I could figure out what it was or who was buried there. We drove past it and into the driveway.

Jim told me about the storm shelter and the possibility of tornados (a thought that had never occurred to me) and then he took me into a small, humble home. There was no TV and only one small radio. Jim told me to turn my shoes upside down to keep the spiders and scorpions out and to always check my bed before getting in. I began to have second thoughts about this "thing called mission." I knew that there were snakes in Oklahoma but I didn't realize that there were so many other "life threatening" obstacles. I uttered a quick prayer asking God to keep all of these critters away from me and not even let me see one!

I had only been in Oklahoma for two weeks when the first threat of violent weather came. They told everyone in Carnegie (thirty miles away) to take cover so I decided that was too close for comfort and I ran out to the storm shelter. I reached down, threw open the cover and three scorpions went running. It was dark down in the shelter and I had a sudden vision of getting down there to find that it was the same place the entire neighborhood snakes had taken shelter, I would die down there and it would be weeks before they found me. I quickly decided that I was safer with the tornado and went back into the house.

A few days later, Jim was out to the mission and I had still not heard anything about the fenced grave in the back yard. I had decided that it must belong to a very great chief to be honored in such a way as to be buried here all by himself. I took advantage of the opportunity to speak to Jim and so I asked him who was buried out there in my yard. Jim looked puzzled and asked me what I was talking about. I explained that there was a fence around a grave in my back yard…it was right there for everyone to see as they drove in the driveway. Jim began to laugh and stated that it was obvious that I had not even walked out there to look at that grave because if I had I would have realized that it was an outdoor baptismal!

Tuesdays were quilting days. The women would arrive about 8:30 in the morning with potluck for lunch and they would sit around a quilt all morning visiting and quilting. The quilts were sold to support the projects at the church and so each one was carefully crafted. The men would come with the women and they would use this time to cut the grass or make repairs on the facilities there. I enjoyed going over to the quilting and I really learned a lot from the women as they shared about their lives, both past and present.

I never could quite get the idea of using a thimble. The women showed me numerous times how to use the thimble to push the needle through the three layers of quilt and to make tiny little stitches but somehow the thimble felt like a bandage to me and so I "protected" that thimble and stabbed my finger continuously. After a few weeks, I began to notice that each Tuesday when we sat down to work on the quilt, all of my stitches were gone.

The parsonage where I lived had a small, portable washing machine but no dryer. Each week I would drag out the washer, fill it full of water and then take my laundry out to the back yard and hang it on the clothesline. One morning, I was hanging out the clothes and I noticed movement a few feet from me. There sat a badger watching me as if he was trying to understand what I was doing. I slowly backed away and told him that I would not bother him, if he would not bother me. Now I had a dilemma, my clothes were out there and I was not sure how I was going to get them. I watched out the window until the badger finally waddled away and sat down on another hill. After that, when I would go out to hang the clothes, the badger would be sitting on a hill on the other side of the driveway watching me. I wonder if he ever figured out what I was doing and if I was doing it right.

I also had a piano in the enclosed front porch. I had played as a young girl, but in my rebellion, I had not touched the piano in several years. There was so little to do during my off time that I decided that I would take up playing again. One evening, as I was playing hymns and singing I became aware of a noise behind me. I was alone in a very remote place and so I became nervous and continued to play hoping that the noise would simply go away. The more I played, the more noise I heard. Finally, I got brave and stopped abruptly. A mother coyote and her cubs were sitting out on the front lawn with their heads thrown back singing hymns to my accompaniment.

WHERE TO NOW LORD?

Leaving seminary was not an easy thing to do. It had been an atmosphere of warmth and support. I loved living in New England and I had really grown in my relationship with God.

I had the promise of a new ministry to look forward to, however, and so I loaded up my belongings and headed for Western New York. I was to be the Director of Christian Education, to minister to those incarcerated in Niagara County and to develop missions on the Tuscarora reservation west of town.

The Tuscarora's were part of the Six Nations and they lived on a small piece of land just outside of Niagara Falls. I knew immediately when I entered the reservation. Poverty was evident in every dwelling.

The church I was to work with was a little mission church that had been abandoned many years earlier, then moved to the reservation. The heat in it was limited, to say the least, and it was in bad need of repair, but the people were as dedicated and caring a group of people as I have ever met.

I remember one winter when the church needed to buy propane to keep the heat on. I was sitting beside Mary Lou as they passed the offering plate. I put something in and passed it to Mary Lou. Mary Lou lived in a rundown house with no running water and no electricity. She did not work and she had no transportation. She heated the living room in the house by hot coal in a coffee can.

Mary Lou reached into her purse and took out $35.00 and put it in the offering plate. Now $35.00 was a lot of money in those days. I couldn't believe it! I asked her later how she could afford to put $35.00 in the offering plate when she had a hard time most months feeding her two children. She told me that she had been saving all year to buy a winter coat, but when the Church needs the money, then that becomes a priority. She quoted me the scripture that says:

> *"Lay not your riches in material possessions, but rather lay them up in spiritual things for they will last forever."*
> *(1 Timothy 5).*

This was a lesson in giving that I have never forgotten.

MY RETURN TO OKLAHOMA

After four and a half years of ministry in Western New York, I accepted a position as the Campus Minister at Bacone College in Muskogee, Oklahoma. Bacone was an American Baptist two year college that focused on American Indians. It didn't take long for me decide that campus ministry was not where I wanted to be. I really didn't know exactly what I wanted to do but I knew I didn't want a pulpit ministry and I obviously didn't want campus ministry, either.

I had decided to leave the ministry and see if there was a way I could serve Indian People in the secular world when I received a phone call from an acquaintance of mine asking me if I was interested in working at a small mission fifty miles from Muskogee. She told me it was a project of the United Methodist Church and they had not had a missionary for almost two years. I agreed to drive out and look at the place and she told me who to contact if I was interested.

I had been in ministry for seven years now and in all of that time I had lived in parsonages. My furniture was blue but every parsonage I had lived in had avocado green carpet. I also owned two horses and two dogs and it was going to be very difficult to find a place that would accommodate my animals. I remember offering a "fleece" to God. I would go anywhere in ministry but my sign of His calling was that the parsonage would have blue carpeting and there would be a place for my animals.

The following weekend I drove out to Cookson, Ok to investigate the possibilities of ministry there. I had to drive over two single lane bridges. I didn't realize that the second bridge was only big enough for one car and I nearly ran an oncoming car off into the creek below. That was no way to start out a new ministry!

As I topped the hill that announced that I was entering the town of Cookson, I became alert to my surroundings. I passed a United Methodist Church, a general store on the left, a Post Office and a small complex of four buildings that were posted as The Cookson Hills Mission. I continued to drive another seven miles in an attempt to find the town.. .that was the town. I finally turned around, came back, and walked around the mission. It seemed abandoned. Chairs were blowing around an empty lot out back, the buildings were all locked up and there was not a soul around.

I decided that the location was acceptable so I called the contacts that I had been given. I was sent an application and arrangements were made for me to see the place. The second time I went to Cookson, I was greeted by a staff person and was given a tour. We went into the parsonage and to my amazement the living room had a blue braided rug on the floor. I dared to ask the question about my horses and my dogs and I was told that there were five acres out back, if I wanted to fence it I could put my horses on it. Everyone out here had a dog.

"Yes Lord! I will go. "

TODAY'S NEED FOR MISSION

I was speaking in a large church. They had extended the invitation for me to come and share my story of the mission where I was assigned and the efforts that are going on there. At the end of my presentation a man raised his hand during the question and answer time. I called on him and he asked me in a voracious voice, "Why do we need mission today? And why do we need it here?"

I hate it when people put me on the defensive and I must struggle to maintain my credibility. I was, after all, a missionary. This was supposed to be about what I was doing...what God was doing through the efforts of this ministry...not whether I *should* be doing it.

From the time of Paul there have been sporadic and individual efforts to make changes in the lives of people through the spreading of the Gospel and the response to the human condition. Christians have long held the belief that turning one's will and life over to the care of God and entering into a personal relationship with our Creator makes life not only tolerable, but enjoyable and fills us with a hope that human life is only the beginning of this relationship. God has given us tools to set the world right and the mandate to respond through our prayers, presence, and our resources, to those the world has ignored or beaten up.

In the late 1700's, William Carey was chosen by "Divine Providence" to set into motion a wide spread and grand missionary movement. Missionary Societies were established and support came from Christians throughout the "civilized" world as the church began to be pervaded by the notion that the Gospel was for every human being.

Throughout the centuries that followed, individuals have felt that God has called them to respond with love and the gospel to places where the "church" either couldn't go or wouldn't go. The church has maintained an interest through the giving of its resources, its prayers and its contacts.

This is a mandate by both the Prophets of old:

> "Is this not the fast that I choose? To lose the chains of injustice and untie the cords of the yoke, to set the oppressed free and break every yoke? Is it not to share your food with the hungry and to provide the poor wanderer with shelter and when you see the naked, to clothe him?... (Isaiah 58: 6-14)

and Jesus, himself:

> *"For I was hungry and you gave me something to eat, I was thirsty and you gave me something to drink, I was a stranger and you invited me in, I was naked and you clothed me, I was in prison and you visited me...Whatever you did for one of the least of these brothers of mine, you did for me." (Matthew 25: 35-40)*

Everybody in the church knows this, it is commonly used anytime the topic of mission is introduced.

The world has become a much smaller place through the media and travel and the inevitable question was raised to me once again... "Why do we need mission today? And why do we need it here?"

Well, I had been to seminary, I had studied the missionary movement, I had been called. I had a well thought out and seasoned response for him and I was just getting ready to sling it out to him when something inside of me told me to wait. I could have made a great argument on historic principals, on biblical principles, but I was acutely aware that this man probably already knew all of that and he was seeking a more personal response from me. I thought about it for a few minutes and then I told him that I would have to think about that and get back to him, but I would get back to him.

The question haunted me over the next week as I went about my work but I continued to ask God for answers. After all, why do we need mission today? And why do we need it here?

Our world is a wealth of information and as I read, as I spoke to others, as I listened to television, I began to hear things that formed an answer to this question for me. I heard that the United States, today, makes up only 20% of the world's population but it consumes 82% of the world's goods. This is not to be mistaken with 82% of its own goods leaving 18% for the rest of the world...82% of everything produced in the world is consumed by Americans. I heard that for every American in this land there are three guns. We are not the safest country in the world, we are the most violent. I heard that one out every three girls can expect to be sexually abused before they are eighteen, usually by someone they know and often by a family member. I heard that one out of every ten people is chemically addicted and that for every church in this country there are seven crack houses. I heard that more than 2 million babies were aborted last year and 1,500 children in this country were murdered by their own mothers.

38,000 children died yesterday…38,000 children will die today…38,000 children will die tomorrow of starvation and malnutrition while Americans spent $16 billion last year on diet foods and another $110 billion for fast food in 2001.

I heard that we don't have a church overcrowding problem in this country, we have a prison overcrowding problem……….. "why do we need mission today? And why do we need it here?"

And so I write this book so that Christians can bear witness that the sharing of the Gospel works to change peoples' lives. I write this book so that Christians can once again have a story to tell to one another. I write this book so that Christians can laugh with and love the brothers and sisters they have in Christ, in places where the church either cannot or will not go.

CHAPTER TWO

"A friend loves at all times..."
PROVERBS 17:17

DESSIE'S STORY

I met Dessie sixteen years ago, early in my tenure at Cookson Hills Center. She lived in a very remote area with her father, way out in the country. Their house was very small and had originally been only two rooms, with a kitchen and bathroom added later on. It was built many years ago and had a worn out tin roof and asphalt siding. The doors hung at an angle, the window casings were rotten, and the front porch was caving in. The only electric service in the house was a single breaker with service to two lights and one outlet. Although there was a well, with water lines to the house, the pump was disabled. There was no running water.

Dessie's father received a Social Security check and took care of both of their needs. Dessie was terrified of people. She never left the house. I frequently took Christmas gifts and food boxes to their home and checked to see if they were all right, but I seldom saw Dessie until five years ago when her father died, leaving her to fend for herself. I would go by the house occasionally to see that she had wood, or to take her something. She would open the door just wide enough to tell me she was alright.

Dessie had shelter and she received a small stipend check of $146.00/month.

A year ago a series of incidents happened that would throw our lives together in a way that would change us both in dramatic ways. An agency in the area decided they were going to pay to build Dessie a new house, and they wanted us to use our volunteers to build it. We readily agreed and began to plan the type of house that would best suit this situation.

Bureaucracy being what it is, we soon realized that Dessie was just another project to them. They were unwilling to make the kinds of adjustments in their approach that were necessary for working in this arena. We told them trust was essential to the project, and no one should approach her alone. They absolutely should not tell her that she would have to move from her house to complete this project. Ignoring our advice they did exactly that. She refused their offer for a new house and would not allow anyone else to come onto her property.

I began to receive phone calls almost immediately from people asking what to do next. I decided to go to Dessie's and talk to her. I loaded up a box of groceries and some pop, and drove to her house. She did allow me to approach her, but she would not come out of the house, so I sat down on the edge of the porch and she stood behind the cracked door. I told her that I was very disappointed, for her, that she was not going to have a new house, but her decision would not keep me from coming to visit her. I determined that she was a child of God in desperate need of human contact. I would visit her at least once a week, just to love her, with no strings attached.

The weather turned bad, but I went every week with a hot meal and pop. I noticed that the only jacket she had was a nylon wind breaker, and she always had the same jeans on. I often arrived at twilight when the light was on in her front room and I could see into the house. There was a wood stove in the middle of the room, a very old bed with a single blanket on it. There was a ragged old vinyl couch and chair sat in the corner.

I became concerned when her wood pile began to shrink and so I asked her if I could send some wood to her. She said yes. Rusty took her a half cord, and while she never opened the door, she knew he was there.

When Christmas arrived, the Canterbury Chapel went Christmas Caroling at her house and took her a plate of cookies. I took her a gift and a food box from the Cookson Hills Center, and every week I arrived with a hot meal and pop.

As winter turned to spring, I noticed that the door began to open a little wider and a little wider each time, until I could see her entire body. Finally, she began to come out on the porch to meet me. She was a beautiful woman, but way too thin and she continued to be very timid. I wondered what else we could do to reach this abandoned little woman.

One rather warm day in the late spring, as I stood in Dessie's front yard, I looked around and noticed that the grass had grown very tall. There was no path to her outhouse and the Johnson grass was waist deep. I am a person who is very concerned with snakes, so I asked her what she was going to do with her grass. "You will have snakes," I told her.

"I know," she replied, "but I don't know what to do."

"Do you want me to come cut your grass?" I asked.

"You?" she asked, hesitantly.

"Yes," I assured.

"OK," she said.

At that point, I felt hope like the touch of Christ's robe. She finally broke through and was trusting me enough to allow me to do something besides bring her a weekly meal. I felt very hopeful, myself, so I decided to pursue her trust a little. With caution, I asked her if she walked on her porch. It was about to collapse and was obviously dangerous. She said that she did sometimes. I warned her about an area that looked extremely bad. Then I quietly raised the question of the porch. "Do you want me to fix the porch?"

Again, she wanted to know if it would be me who fixed the porch. I assured her that it would be me. I was so excited that I wanted to scream, but I was pretty sure that would scare her right back into the house, so I settled for telling her I would get right on it. I sang all the way back to the Center, "God is good all the time, He put a song of praise in this heart of mine...."

As spring turned to early summer, I found myself down at Dessie's several times; I kept her grass mowed, she allowed the men to bring down my tractor and brush hog her path, we put a new tin roof on her outhouse, and we rebuilt her front porch. The more I was there, the easier it was to talk to her. I always made time to visit, but she still was very hesitant to let me do much.

Finally, I asked her what was wrong with her water. She told me that a man had come twenty years ago, taken a part of the pump, and never returned. I surmised that there couldn't be anything terribly wrong with her water if it was only a small part. "Would you let me bring a friend down to look at your water?" I asked.

"Yeah," came the reply.

Discussions unfolded about the best way to fix the water with the brittle and broken pipes into the old part of the house, and whether the well was safe. I asked Dessie if I could go into the house to look at the bathroom and the kitchen. I was shocked by what I saw. The roof had caved in, the floor had fallen six inches. The drain for the toilet stood in the middle of the floor, while the toilet lay on its side where it had obviously fallen over. The bathtub was cracked from lack of use, and the hot water tank had never been used. The kitchen was filthy; water and dampness were everywhere, and rodent droppings were an inch deep. There was an old wood cook stove in the corner, but the roof had caved in on it and it was piled high with insulation.

"Dessie," I said, "even if I get the well fixed, there is no place to go with the water. We will have to fix the kitchen and the bathroom for them to work. Will you let me do that?"

She hesitated. About that time, Rusty finished some mowing he was doing and called me over. He told me that he had been looking at the back of the house. It was about to cave in. He was pretty sure it could not be repaired, and even if we could, it would never look right. "Let's ask her if she will let us put on an addition," he said. "I could add a kitchen and a bathroom on the end of the house. Tell her we will put a doorway through where the window is when everything else is done. She will never have to leave her house, and we won't have to come in to the old part if she doesn't want us to.

"OK," she told me, "as long as you are here."

Volunteer In Mission teams were lined up, materials purchased and plans made. We would add on a 14x24 foot kitchen and bathroom, with a porch across the front and a door out the back. There would be adequate lights and outlets. There would be water. We would put a new roof on the old and new alike, and the old house would be sided. She even consented to let us tear off the nasty bathroom and kitchen to return the house to the original structure. I was thrilled, but I was also afraid that, at any point, she could get scared and shut us out. I prayed that God would continue to give Dessie the courage to let us help her.

God always goes ahead of us when we ask. We arrived at the house the first day of the project with five workers. I got there early to reassure her and to make sure she was going to allow us to start. The team pulled up and began digging the holes for the corner posts. We had not been there more than twenty minutes when a local power company truck drove up. The company had decided that it was time to take the electric meters off all houses and put them on poles. This would necessitate a drop loop and new cable into the house and since it was their NEW policy, they were going to pay for it. We knew that we were going to have to replace the box and we'd intended to add a drop loop and put the cable underground. It was going to mean a savings to us of about $800.00!

Cherokee Nation jumped in to help with materials, and then they decided they were going to put in her water. Another agency in town agreed to blow insulation into her crawl space. One of our volunteers was so touched with her story that he went to town one day and bought a brand new refrigerator, stove, hot water tank and heater and donated them to our project.

As things began falling into place, Dessie began to show signs of being excited. I asked her what she was most anxious for. She told me that she washed out of a little aluminum dish pan on the woodstove. She had not had a bath in twenty years, and had NEVER had a hot bath. I vowed that we would not stop working until she had a bathtub and hot water, and I was personally buying her a bottle of bubble bath.

Canterbury Chapel United Methodist Women decided to have a housewarming for her, so the President went with me to talk with her about curtains and bath rugs. She wanted colors and she needed to see what Dessie needed. When asked about dishes, Dessie told her that she ate off a paper plate and she had a plastic fork. When asked about clothes, Dessie said that she had no winter coat, two pairs of jeans, and two tee shirts; one she washed while wearing the other. They collected dishes, pots and pans, silverware, curtains, blankets, rugs, a washing machine, furniture and clothing.

The story of Dessie is *not* a story about what we were able to build her. It is *not* a story about what we were able to provide her. Dessie's story is not a story about what people bought her or even of how her standard of living was raised. Dessie's story is of a person who lived a lonely and hopeless life with no human contact to speak of. It is the story of a woman who had no resources and no knowledge of the services that could help her. She lived day to day, wondering who in the world cared about her, until one day she reached out to the people of God, touched the hem of the garment of Christ, and trusted that somehow she would be helped.

It is the story of a woman who has grown throughout this process, a woman who would barely open her front door in the beginning, and now greets everyone who comes to her door with a smile and a welcome. A woman who now lets us know her needs and wants us to help her, a woman who asks us to *take her to town*. God has performed miracles in her life, using only a housing project to do it. One morning one of the staff here at Cookson said to me, "That is not the same woman as two months ago." The *real* story of Dessie is that a woman had just enough faith to reach out to the people of God, and He responded compassionately to her through those same people.

Dessie died just ten days after we completed her house. We were the ones to find her body and we saw to it that it was taken care of. She died too soon but she died knowing that there was a God and He loved her so much that He sent His people to love her too.

The story does not end there, however, for those of us who have had the privilege of knowing Dessie have also experienced the power of God. We were reminded of why it is important for the church to respond to the needs of people, and not leave it up to other agencies that must adhere to policies and procedures. It was only because we were able to go to Dessie's house on a weekly basis, regardless of whether she ever even opened the door for us. We do this because every human needs to experience the *unconditional* love of Christ. We are the arms, we are the hearts that share this love with others. God continues to work with us every time we reach out, with a little faith, and touch the hem of His garment. We are expected to do no less.

MR. C

I was told that in my visitations, I needed to go and see Mr. C. He was a Senior Citizen, so I asked our Senior Citizen's Director to make a visit out to his home and invite him to come to the lunches we were serving at the Mission.

The directions were clear as she drove out to the residence of Mr. C. It was way out in the country. It would have been very difficult to find for anyone who was not familiar with the area. When she pulled into the driveway, the only structure there was a beat up old travel trailer. She got out of the car and went up to the door. After several knocks, she heard a man's voice calling, "come in." What she found upon entering the residence would leave even the most calloused person feeling the pain of poverty and injustice.

Mr. C. had no legs. He had lost them to diabetes. The trailer was too small for a wheelchair so Mr. C. dragged himself around when he needed to get something or use the bathroom. He had no running water, so the place was dirty. He had to depend on people to bring him water and if they didn't show up he simply went without. He had no transportation, no means of paying his bills (he received a disability check, but one must be able to get to the mailbox). He was totally dependent on others to meet his most basic needs.

Mr. C. was a simple man who had lived in the country his whole life. He did not know about the agencies and systems that could help him. We located a house close to his trailer, built a ramp and saw to it that the water was turned on. We helped him get established in the house and connected him with providers who could come and assist him with the basic needs of his life. Mr. C. lived two years with the help of others, knowing that there were people in this world who are anxious to make life a little easier in every way that they could.

TAKING EASTER TO THE DOCTOR

I had not been at Cookson very long when we decided to have a Thanksgiving Dinner for the Senior Citizen's. I was told that I would have to go out to every home, tell them about the dinner, go on the day of the dinner to pick them up, and after the dinner take everyone back home again. I began my journey to tell everyone we would like to host them the following day and what time I would be there to transport them.

I arrived at a small log house with a tumble down roof and extremely shaky steps. I knocked on the door and a rather weak voice invited me to come on in Cherokee. I opened the door and went in. There lay Easter in an old four-poster bed, looking very sick. Her granddaughter sat beside her and translated for her (Easter spoke very little English). I asked her what was wrong and her granddaughter told me that she was having trouble breathing. I asked if her grandmother had been to the doctor. Yes, she said, three times but they would tell her to go home and use her nebulizer (a machine that helped her breath). They were very poor and could not afford the fifty-mile trip to the hospital in town any more.

"Are you using the nebulizer?" I asked.

"It doesn't work," her granddaughter responded.

"What do you mean?" I asked.

"There is something wrong with it. Every time we plug it in it blows a fuse." Her granddaughter told me.

I looked at the light fixture in the ceiling. It was a single bulb with a pull chain. There was a connector between the bulb and the fixture and at least five cords plugged into the connector. I then looked at the nebulizer. The plug on it was burned. I told the young woman not to plug it in again, it was dangerous. I added that if her grandmother was not feeling any better the next day when I came by with the van, I would take her to the doctor myself.

The day of the dinner was overcast, but pleasant. I loaded up in the van and began to make my rounds. I arrived at Easter's and her granddaughter met me at the road. "Grandma's real sick," she told me. I went inside and found Easter in the bed, too weak to get up. I wrapped her in a blanket and carried her out to the van. We gave her a seat of her own so that she could lie down and we headed back to Cookson to drop the others off for dinner. I gave instructions to the staff to take care of the dinner and then to take everyone back home. I headed to town.

I arrived at the hospital and carried Easter into the emergency room. I was met at the door by an irate nurse who told me that they could not see Easter again. They had treated her three times and there was nothing else they could do. She needed to go home and use her nebulizer.

"It doesn't work!" Her granddaughter told her.

"You haven't used it long enough," came the reply.

"No!" I intervened, "you don't understand. The nebulizer is broken. There is no using it at all." I went on to tell this nurse that Easter lived almost fifty miles from the hospital and it was a tremendous stress on her to have to make the trip over and over to see a doctor. Further, she lived in a very drafty house with wood heat. Her respiratory problems would not be solved there.

I finally convinced them to treat her. They drew blood for some tests. Within a few minutes they were rushing around, admitting her into the Intensive Care Unit with pneumonia. She recuperated in the hospital for ten days.

The lesson for me in this story was a simple one. When we are communicating with each other, it is important that we understand, totally, what the other person is trying to say. "It doesn't work" can be understood to mean that it isn't helping or that it is broken. Making the assumption that it meant "it isn't helping" almost cost Easter her life.

TIFFANY AND BILLY

When I was in Lockport, New York, I served a large church as the Director of Christian Education and Missions. One of my delights was to go to the Niagara County Jail and hold a Bible Study every week.

One week while I was visiting the jail I met a young woman who was being held on prostitution charges. I asked her if there was anything that I could do for her and she asked me if I could check on her kids for her.

"Does the Department of Human Services know that you have kids?" I asked.

"No," she responded, "and please don't tell them. If they find out that I have kids they will take them away from me and I will never get them back. Besides, they are OK, they just don't know where I am. I just need someone to go and tell them that I will make bond tomorrow and then I'll be home."

I was a little hesitant to go to the home of this woman, but I decided that I should tell her kids where she was so I obtained the address from her and drove over there. I was young and naive and truly believed that I would go to this apartment and find two teenage kids taking care of themselves, needing only for someone to tell them where their mother was.

I arrived at the apartment building in a rundown section of town, went to the door and knocked. At the second knock, the door of the apartment across the hall flew open and an irate woman exclaimed, "Its about time that someone came and checked on those kids. Where have you been for the past three days?"

I tried to explain to her that I was only there to report the whereabouts of their mother and then I would be on my way. I told her that the kids had not opened the door for me to talk to them.

"And they won't," she said with contempt. She stepped inside her apartment and got a key to the apartment I was visiting and opened door. When we went in I discovered that the kids I was to check on were not teenagers at all, they weren't even elementary age, they were three years and eighteen months old. The baby had not had his diaper changed in three days and they were dressed only in underwear.

Since I had promised *not* to tell the authorities about these kids without gathering some information first, I found some blankets, wrapped them up against the New York winter weather and took them with me. The woman in the apartment across the hall assumed that I was within my authority to do this and was, frankly, glad to see them go.

Billy, the baby, had a sweet personality. He was hungry and so the first order of the day was to take them home and feed them. I made some potatoes and gravy for him, set it on his highchair tray and turned to get his sister, Tiffany, something to eat. When I turned back around he had taken the bowl of potatoes and gravy and dumped them on his head. It's been too long, I thought to myself. I cleaned up the mess, fed him, bathed him and put him to bed.

Then I turned my attention to his sister, who had been giving me "helpful hints" throughout the ordeal. Tiffany was the most beautiful child I had ever laid my eyes on. She had a rich auburn colored hair that hung in ringlets to her shoulders. Her eyes were emerald green, but she had the mouth of a hooker.

I had picked the children up on Friday night so on Saturday I called the jail to see what time their mother was to make bail. I was told that she was not going to be able to over the weekend so I loaded up the kids into my car and went to K-Mart. I knew that I would need diapers, and some church clothes since they would be with me over a Sunday.

I bought Billy a little suit and I bought Tiffany a dress, complete with ruffles, and a little pair of patent leather shoes. The following morning I dressed them in their new clothes and took them to Sunday School I dropped Billy off in the nursery and took Tiffany to the 2-3 year old class. I was teaching the adult class, so I explained the circumstances for her presence and went to my class.

Soon after my opening prayer, we were interrupted by a knock at the door. There stood the Sunday School Teacher with Tiffany by the hand. "Do you know what this child said?" She asked in horror.

"No," I replied, "but leave her here, she will only be here today. I sat Tiffany in the corner with a pencil and a piece of paper and proceeded with my class.

As the week progressed it became clear that I would have the kids with me for another Sunday so we began to discuss "Sunday School language". The next Sunday, I dressed the kids in their good clothes and I took them to Sunday School. I went to my adult class and had just gotten started when we were interrupted by a knock at the door. There stood the Sunday School teacher, again, with Tiffany by the hand.

"She said it again!" She exclaimed.

"Leave her here," I told her. I sat Tiffany in the corner with a pencil and paper and proceeded with my class. The following week we made a real concentrated effort to change the "hooker" language into "Sunday School language" and when Sunday rolled around again I dressed the kids with confidence. Today they would be alright in Sunday School.

I dropped Tiffany off in her class and as I was making my way to my class I heard someone calling me as they ran down the hall. Yes, it was the teacher with Tiffany in tow. When she caught me she said, "She said it again! We can't have this, she is influencing all the other children. You simply can't leave her in Sunday School anymore."

I took Tiffany with me to my class and I pulled her up into my lap. As I gazed down into that precious, beautiful little head I prayed, "God, oh God, why is it that one child can influence twenty children, but twenty children can't influence the one?"

THAT'S SCARY

They were elderly and living on a limited fixed income. She was legally blind. They had no car, no telephone. They barely had enough to eat. They were afraid that someone would come to their house to rob them or hurt them, so William sat by the window with a shotgun in his lap after dark.

One night, William got sick. It was his heart. It was two miles to the next house and it was dark. His wife tried to go to call an ambulance but she got lost. What a long night that was for them, her wandering around in the woods, him suffering a heart attack. She was worried sick about him, he was worried about her. Help came in the morning and they were able to get William to the hospital, but it was clear to me that these people needed a telephone. I began to make phone calls and arrangements for service to their home.

A friend of mine had recently died and her family had given me her phone. She was also "vision challenged" and the phone had large numbers on it. I was so excited to give this phone to this couple who needed help.

A few weeks after William was released from the hospital, I decided to visit. I was sitting in their living room when I noticed that the jacks were there for the phone, but the phone was missing. When I asked what happened, I was told that the phone rang one night. It startled William since he had never had a phone in his house. Without thinking he grabbed the shot gun and shot the phone! Once again, they were without a phone.

How often we destroy the very things in our lives that could give us help and support! For William, it was the phone, for others of us it is our bodies, or our relationships, or our faith. How wonderful to serve a God who not only knows this but is always ready to re-establish a connection with us when we are ready to use it.

WHERE'S MY MOMMY?

For all intents and purposes, this was to be a normal delivery baby girl. Nine months had passed, we had given a baby shower, the room was ready, and everyone was excited. Dana went into labor on Thursday, and everyone was called. "It's time, it's time." We all anxiously waited for the phone to ring announcing the arrival of this new child. The call came, but it was NOT what everyone expected. Dana had something called placenta prevail, there was too much blood, she had been taken by life flight helicopter to a hospital in Tulsa. No one knew anything more.

We left for Tulsa immediately and sat with the family all night and into the next day. The doctors were running tests, but Dana was definitely on life support. Finally, the doctor came in to speak to the family; there was no response, no brain activity. It was time to make a decision, did they want to say their last goodbyes?

This is one of the hardest times to be a Pastor. Attention turned to me, what did I think? What should they do? I walked the long hall with Dana's husband and we entered her room. She was lying there, eyes shut, not moving, only the sounds of the machines around her. It wasn't supposed to be this way. She was so young and healthy. This was supposed to be a glorious celebration. The baby was fine, how could this happen? I secretly prayed all of these questions as I begged God to show me how to deal with this devastated family.

The young father told me that his four year old daughter didn't seem to understand what was going on. He asked me to talk to her. I don't like to tell children things like, God needed your mommy more than you did, or she is with God now. That sets God up for some undeserved anger and resentments. God doesn't take people away, He receives them when their bodies fail. Every human body will fail eventually, and I want children to know that God takes care of them when that happens, but God doesn't cause it to happen. Birth is the beginning of life, death is simply the end of it.

We entered the room where her mother lay. I watched the child tell her mommy that they were going to go home now and she would see her tomorrow. She had on a tee shirt with a Lion King picture on the front.

"Did you see the movie Lion King?" I asked her.

"Yes," she said, "it is my favorite!"

"Do you remember when Simba's daddy got trampled by the water buffalo and went away. And then later he came back in the stars and told Simba that he was up in the stars watching him?"

She dropped her head and quietly said, "Yes".

"Your mommy is going to be watching you from the stars, too." I told her. "Your mommy must go away and not come back, but she will be close. She loves you very much." The child began to sob and cling to her mother and I knew that she now understood what was happening.

Three days later we buried Dana. Her little family sat in the front row, her four year old daughter and her loving husband holding their four day old baby. The four year old sat through the funeral with silent resignation until the funeral directors came up to open the coffin at the end of the service. When the child saw her mommy lying there, she ran up to her, grabbed her hand and pleaded, "Get up mommy! Get up! I don't want you to go away, I don't want you to live in the stars. Get up Mommy! PLEASE!"

I sobbed as they carried the child out of the room. How do we handle death, if we don't know that God has created a plan for eternal life? How do we deal with death if we don't understand it? How do we go on if we don't have the hope that God created life as a beginning, not an end in itself?

No funeral is ever easy. It doesn't matter how old a person is or how long loved ones have had to prepare, death is hard. I am so grateful that this lonely separation is only temporary.

GOD'S PROMISES FULFILLED

I met her eighteen years ago at an AA meeting. She waltzed into the room with her demeanor swirling all around her. She breezed up to the table and gave an enthusiastic "hello" to anyone who gave her any attention. She had on a purple hat, a red gypsy blouse, and tan colored pants. She was far more dramatic than I was comfortable with, and I really wondered what she was doing there.

When the meeting was over, she came up, introduced herself to me, and invited me to go for coffee with several of the others. I am not sure why I accepted, but I did. Over the months that followed, we became friends and I learned what a deep spirituality this woman had. She had been addicted to alcohol and to "black mollies and white crosses," a form of speed, for almost twenty years. At the time I met her she'd been sober nine months.

As the months and years unfolded, I learned to depend upon this woman for support in any venture I made with alcoholics and addicts. She was a Charter member of the Cookson 12-Step group, she was a Charter member of the Canterbury 12-Step Church, she helped start meetings at the church and throughout the surrounding communities.

Her story unfolded slowly. I'd gathered bits and pieces from conversations, but it was not until I heard her speak at an AA Meeting one night that I was able to put together the full story.

She came from an upstanding family in the community. Her father was a politician and her mother was the mayor of her home town. She played trumpet in the band and had played on tour in Europe. Her father died when she was fifteen. She had been active in the church her entire life. One Sunday night shortly after her dad's death, she skipped the church youth activity and went for a joy ride with a friend. She was driving without a license on a dirt road when the truck spun out of control. Her face hit the steering wheel, knocking out all of her teeth and disfiguring her face. Recovery took several years, to replace her teeth so that she could play the trumpet again, and to rebuild her face. There was an abundance of pain medication to go along with all of the dental and medical work she was receiving. She felt that the accident was God's punishment for not being at church where she belonged. Her discomfort with God intensified as the drugs became more and more of a problem, and at some point she decided that God was going to send her to hell anyway, so why try?

She got pregnant in her second year of college, a time in our history when pregnancy outside of marriage was simply not tolerated. She was sent away to deal with her guilt and shame, and the baby was put up for adoption in another state. I'd known her for six years before she told me about the pregnancy. She never talked about it, but there was always a haunted look on her face whenever someone appeared with a new baby.

She came to me and told me the story once again. As she finished she said, "I think I want to find her, just to make sure that she is alright, and to give her any medical history that she might need to have." We prayed about it that night, and we added this concern to our prayers for several months. Finally, she was ready to begin the search. Her child was twenty six years old.

She consolidated the information she had with the information that her brother knew. Even the date of birth was undetermined. The hospital was unable to find any record of her having been admitted around the date that she remembered. She contacted the adoption agency that had handled the adoption, and they told her they could give her "unidentifiable" information only. She asked them to send her anything they could, the "unidentifiable information" included a date of birth and the first names of the adoptive parents.

It looked hopeless. At Bible Study that night we all prayed that if it were time for her to find her child, God would open the necessary doors. When she arrived home the phone was ringing. A friend had been on the internet, at a website where adoptive children and parents can register, their searches for each other. There was a woman born on the exact date, in the same city, with the same adoptive parents' unique first names. She had begun her search just two weeks prior to Elsie's. If Elsie had begun looking any earlier, it would have been futile.

God's timing is always perfect! God has promised that when we return to Him, we will begin to see the goodness of life unfold. I am not implying that God will give us everything that we want, or that all of life suddenly develops a happy ending, but when God is involved and a miracle does happen...what a joy! What a thrill! What a testimony to the power and concern of the God we serve.

Two months after Elsie began the search for her child, they were reunited and have had the opportunity to develop a relationship...a relationship much different than parent to child, but one that is strong and valuable to each of them.

ADA

She was a tiny woman who spoke very little English. Her first language was Cherokee. Her home was small and it had a lot of problems. She had come to the Center to ask us to help her fix her bathroom floor. It seems that the floor was rotting around the tub, and it was caving in.

When I arrived at the house to assess the damage and get a materials list, I noticed a quilt frame hanging from the ceiling in the living room. Immediately my thoughts went back to a story my dad had told me about how my Grandmother had hung a quilt from the ceiling. It was on ropes, he told me. The women would lower the quilt to lap height when they were quilting, and when they are done working on it, they would pull the ropes and raise it up out of the way. I never could visualize this method of quilting until I saw Ada's quilt.

We visited for quite a while and decided that we would fix the floor in the bathroom, as well as replace her leaky roof and rebuild her dangerous porch. I told her we would be there the first of the week with a group to get started. I always ask the homeowner to be there while we are working, and to supply the team with cold water to drink. I assured her that this work and the materials were gifts from the United Methodist Church.

Monday arrived and we loaded up the tool trucks with materials and supplies. We worked all day stripping the shingles off her roof and putting new ones down. The next day we arrived, ready to continue our project, but Ada would not open the door. I knocked, but she refused to answer. Finally, she told us to go away.

"Miss Ada," I called, "we must finish your roof, there are no shingles on it, it will never shed water."

Finally, in desperation, she came to the door. "What's wrong?" I asked. It seems that after we had loaded up the previous day, a black truck with two men came to the house. They came to the door and told her they were from the Cookson Hills Center, and that she owed $800.00 for the work we had done. They told her we would not come back to finish the job until she paid them. They had come into her house and threatened her until she finally gave them all of the cash she had ($30.00) just to get rid of them. She told them she would have the rest of it the next day.

She was terrified and I was furious! I assured her that she didn't owe us anything. I told her that if they came back, to simply tell them that she had already paid me. We called the police and we staked out her house, but we never did find the men who would do such a low-down thing.

VICTOR

One of the people who influenced me the most in my early years as a missionary was a Kiowa man named Victor. Victor was a Pastor with the American Baptist Church and he served his people as a voice between Traditional Kiowas and Christians. Victor was a Christian but he was highly respected in both camps.

Upon my arrival in Western Oklahoma, I was told by the missionaries already there that Christians did NOT go to Pow-Wows. I was told that the Indian People did not want us there and that it would negatively affect my Christian witness. I was disturbed by this because I believed that I was my Christian witness no matter where I was, but I was learning so I did not question their philosophy.

Victor, however, felt that part of the cultural experience was to learn how to dance even if you never used it. So once a week he would come to my house and teach me how to round-dance, gourd-dance, two-step, and war dance. It was during these times that he subtly taught me many things about the Kiowa People and their history.

Victor had a real sense of humor and it was hard to know when he was telling the truth and when he was pulling your leg. One evening as we were sitting around the table after my "dance lesson," Victor said, "You know, Indians have two names, a Christian name and an Indian name."

I looked for the usual twinkle in his eye that appeared when he was teasing. "No, Victor, I didn't know that," I replied. "But Victor isn't a Christian name or an Indian name." I continued.

"Oh, I know," he said, "I have three names."

A little more convinced, I continued, "What's your Christian name?"

"Luke," Victor said with vigor. "Oh," I said, "I had no idea. I really like the name Luke, Victor, what's your Indian name?"

"Warm water," he said with obvious delight. There was nothing left for me to do but laugh.

One particularly warm evening, Victor and I were sitting in the fellowship hall because there was air conditioning there. I was deep in thought about the Kiowa People and how wonderful they were. I also had just come from seminary and we all know that at that point in a minister's life, we think we know everything.

"Victor," I began, "it seems to me that the only thing wrong with the Indian people is that they worship the wrong god."

Victor sat quietly for several minutes contemplating what I had just said and then he quietly responded, "You mean there's more than one?"

That single little question in response to my arrogance and my ignorance has both changed and formed my theology for some twenty three years now. Whenever I begin to think that I have all of the answers, whenever I begin to think that everyone must respond to God the way that I determine to be correct, then that little phrase comes back to me… "You mean there's more than one?" I have come to believe that there is *only* ONE God and this God is for all people and therefore their way of worship may differ from mine but I am convinced that we have more in common than we have differences.

Yes Victor, there is only one *God. Thank you.*

CHARLIE

I came to the mission field knowing very little about carpentry. It quickly became evident that, here at Cookson, carpentry was going to be a big part of the work that we do. There are so many people who live in substandard housing and we receive many requests for help in making repairs.

I asked Charlie to help me and to teach me. I learned most of what I know about carpentry from Charlie. He loved to take some wood, begin a project, and then say, "This what you had in mind?" I had a hard time visualizing what he was doing and he loved that. He had an eye for line, also. If a wall was a little bit off, he could see it. If a roof line ran down hill, he would tell us. It took me a long time to be able to see with the eyes Charlie saw with.

We were loading up a truck one day with roofing material. The project was about fourteen miles away, down a dirt road, so we wanted to limit our trips back and forth. We put on a pile of wafer board and I asked Charlie if that wasn't a pretty good load. "No," he said, "put some shingles on there, too." We began to load the shingles. "Enough?" I kept asking. We kept loading and finally got to the tools. When we were finished loading, I couldn't see over the dashboard so Charlie drove. We headed out, going slowly and trying to avoid the potholes that were everywhere. We had driven about eleven miles when we hit a little bump in the road and both back tires blew out at the same time. We looked at each other, startled, and said in unison, "Too much load."

Charlie was always playing practical jokes and he especially loved to joke with the work teams. If they asked him a question, he would tell them it would cost them $5.00 for the answer. We were putting skirting on a house one day and Charlie would cut a piece and then watch as the women would work to make it fit. We had come to the last piece. Charlie carried it over to them and squatted down next to the house. Every time the women would try to move the board he would secretly reach out and hold it. They would pull and strain and arrange, and then one of them would go back and dig a little. They would try to fit it again and Charlie would reach out and hold on. They would struggle and strain and then one of them would go back to digging. This went on for no less than ten minutes. They had dug a huge ditch before they realized that the real reason that the piece would not fit was because of Charlie.

Charlie was a good friend and a fisherman. He spent many hours fishing, then would bring the fish to me and we would picnic together. He would ask me to go fishing with him, but I didn't really like to fish. Sometimes I would take a book and try to read, but he would "suggest" that I steer the boat into a cove or hand him something, so I really didn't get much reading done. One day, Charlie decided to fish down by the dam. We had not been there very long when I noticed a large bird being tossed against the wall of the dam. It would go under the water and come back up. I had watched it for several minutes as it struggled. Finally, I said, "Charlie, that duck is drowning." Charlie informed me that ducks don't drown. He went back to his fishing.

"Charlie," I said, "that duck is a little one and it is drowning." He informed me once again that ducks don't drown and went back to fishing.

"Charlie," I said, "let's go over there and make sure."

By this time, Charlie was convinced that he was not going to get any fishing done until we had checked on the duck, so in frustration he guided the boat over to the wall. The closer we got the more it became evident that the bird was in distress. Charlie pulled the boat up alongside it, got his fishing net, and scooped it up out of the water. The "duck" turned out to be a road runner that had apparently been trying to fly across the river and slammed into the wall. It was, indeed, drowning. We took it to shore and turned it loose. It sat there for a few minutes, catching its breath, turned, and started up the hill. When it was a safe distance from us it turned back, gave us a nod, and took off up the hill.

One fall day, we were sitting out by the workshop enjoying the cool weather, when Charlie asked me if I loved him. We had worked closely together for four years, so it was hard for me to imagine that he would even ask me this question.

"Of course I love you, Charlie," I said. "You know that."

"Then how come you never told me about your friend, Jesus?" He asked.

I was flabbergasted! Charlie was a Traditional Indian and I had not wanted to offend him by making him think he had to believe my way. We sat out by the shop for the next three hours talking about Jesus, traditional ways and God. We both learned a lot that day, in our conversations and in our introspection.

A few weeks later I flew to New York to speak. I hugged Charlie and told him to take care of the place. I would see him in two weeks. He hugged me and told me that it would depend on what the "Big Guy" had in mind. That was the last time that I saw Charlie alive. He died, sitting in his chair, five days after I left.

"I WAS IN PRISON AND YOU CAME TO ME"

Working with alcoholics and addicts can put the church in close contact with some of the community's most colorful people. There is one family that came to the church after the father attended services as an activity of the treatment center where he was a resident. The couple attended off and on and when their son was born, they brought him to me to be baptized. As the years passed, drugs continued to plague them. One of them would get clean, but the other one would not, then the tables would turn. They seemed unable to both get clean at the same time.

Rumors flew about drug deals, shootings, methamphetamine labs, and all sorts of sordid activities. Doty had her throat cut, then was shot. Bart was arrested and was serving time with a very long sentence. The children were staying with their grandmother. All was quiet for about six months. Then a phone call came; "There's been a murder next door to me. Somebody just walked up on the porch and shot a woman in the head. I don't know who it is, but it is Doty's house." My heart sank as my friend proceeded to tell me that the children, ages 5 and 3, were home and had apparently witnessed the murder.

I asked whether I should come, but was told that the FBI were everywhere. No one was allowed in or out of the area. I began to pray for the children. I prayed for Doty, I prayed for Bart. I prayed for my frightened friend. Then the call came. It was not Doty, it was her twenty year old babysitter who'd been murdered. I prayed for her family.

People who work closely with alcoholics and addicts often acknowledge that a person must "hit bottom" before they stop drinking and drugging. We all wait for the consequences of chemical dependency to become so painful that the user is willing to go to any length to stop. No one ever knows what determines the final episode, but we all pray that it isn't death.

I prayed that Doty had hit her bottom and was ready to stop, but it was not the case. She continued her addict lifestyle for another year.

In the meantime, I heard reports that her husband, Bart, had found Christ in prison and was working with the chaplain teaching Bible Studies and leading worship. Everyone who knew him said that he'd made a complete and miraculous turn around and was thriving in prison.

Bart told me that the single issue that haunted him was his two children. He prayed for them and asked God to help him stay relevant in their lives, in spite of the fact that he would not be freed until they were grown. He needed to visit with them whenever possible and he sought ways to stay involved in their lives. He had served three years of a 30 year sentence, when a cell mate discussed his case with an attorney friend. Before Bart knew what happened, he'd been released on a technicality. Seeing this release as a gift from God, he came home and took over custody of his children. He began coming to the church again and was faithful in attendance every Sunday, bringing his children to both Sunday School and Church. We were thrilled! We regularly prayed for his wife.

Then the news came that she had checked herself into treatment. She was ready to leave her old life behind and get into recovery. We prayed that this would be the time she would change for good. Thirty days of treatment came and went and we heard rave reviews of her progress.

Upon her release, she came back into our community and tried to piece her life back together. She immersed herself in her family and her church. She came to Bible Study, Sunday School, children's activities, Alcoholics Anonymous, and every other organization that she could lock onto. She was really putting her life back together and everyone was so happy for her and her family.

Doty talked openly about her past as she became more and more comfortable with a drug free life. She would often refer to her "using" days, and how unaware she became in the last year of her addiction. She knew that there might be old warrants and charges filed against her, and she was prepared to deal with the "wreckage of her past."

One Sunday, she was preparing dinner for her family and realized that they were out of bread. She grabbed her purse and headed for the grocery store. As she approached the four way stop sign in the middle of town, she was deep in thought about the turn her life had taken. She rolled through the stop sign. She was pulled over, ticketed and then arrested for on old warrant from another county.

When I was told that she was in jail, I called and asked whether I would be permitted to visit her. I would, if I got down there right away. I drove the forty-five minutes to town and I was taken to the visiting room which was a small area divided by windows. There were three cubicles with telephones, and two doors, one in the room where I was, and one in the room on the other side of the windows.

Doty was escorted into the room on the other side and we picked up the phones. "I can't believe that you are here!" she kept saying. "I can't believe that they let you in! I can't believe that my Pastor is here, my lawyer couldn't even get in. You must have some powerful connections!"

I just smiled as I thought of the "powerful connection" I had. I finally said, "God can do anything."

She began to tell me how she was doing. We didn't discuss the charges, there was no point. She always knew that this was a possibility. Instead, she wanted to tell me what had happened after she was processed.

"I have a room to myself," she began, "so I decided that I would just spend this time by myself, thinking, praying and meditating. Then I remembered the Sunday School lesson we had today. It was about witnessing and sharing our stories, so I got up and went to the recreation room. There are twelve other women in here and I know them all. They all began to ask me where I had been and what I had been doing, so I told them. I told them all about treatment, I told them all about our church and I even think some of them might come after they get out."

There was some confusion about her bail. She spent twelve days in jail when she could have been released within twenty-four hours. But she believes that God had a plan for her in that jail. When she returned to church, she told us that she had shared her faith with several girls, and that they had even started a Bible Study. She said that they really didn't know anything about the Bible, so they just picked a favorite verse and read it. They all spent hours reading the Bible so that they would have a "good" verse to share.

Wouldn't life be wonderful if we could all accept the cards that life deals us, and look for ways to turn bad circumstances into opportunities to serve God?

CHAPTER THREE

"Teach me to do your will, For
You are my God; Let Your good spirit
lead me on level ground."
PSALMS 143:10

THE WITNESS

"Boy, this is going to be a steamer," I said to Rusty as we loaded up the tools and materials for the Volunteer-In-Mission team that had arrived to help with a week of construction work. We were starting a new project and I had not been there yet. "Do you think we will have enough work for ten people?" I asked.

"Oh, I don't think you'll have to look far to find something for them to do," he responded.

We left the Cookson Hills Center, drove north about ten miles and then headed east on a dirt road. The first house on the dirt road was a big, impressive two story house with a glass enclosure around an indoor pool. The gardens were beautiful and meticulously kept. I had not seen such a house in this part of the country and was impressed that after fifteen years of traveling the hills of Cherokee County, there were still places that I was not aware of. I sat back in the seat and looked out at the rolling hills and the beauty of eastern Oklahoma, enjoying the wind as it blew in the window. I knew that in a very short time the temperature would be what we call "smokin' hot" in this part of the country.

We rounded a bend and I couldn't believe my eyes. The woods turned to meadows and there was a group of extravagant buildings. I gazed at stables, with cobblestone floors, that were as big as our gym. A greenhouse, huge garages, a multi-million dollar house with landscaping, gardens, and a manmade creek running through it with rock bridges crossing it. I sat up straight and gave a soft whistle. "Who lives here?" I asked.

Rusty, a native of this area, told me that it belonged to a family who had a business not far from the Center; a business that employees the poor, pays them minimum wage and lays them off with every change of season.

The next group of houses were ones that I was more familiar with. The sides were covered with tar paper and the roofs were tin. They are lovingly re-ferred to as "shotgun houses" in Oklahoma. I began to wonder how a family with so much, one that had obtained their riches on the backs of these humble people, could live in all that luxury right next door to families who have such a difficult struggle. Driving past these homes every day and then arriving at the home of Randy and Carol was a real stretch to my theology.

As we pulled up in front of the house I would be working on for the next three weeks, I began to feel a little more comfortable. This was the type of home that we frequented. The siding was tar paper, the roof was warped and

46

badly in need of shingles. The inside had not been painted in thirty years and the walls were covered in soot. The chimney was caving in, there was no water in the kitchen, and the septic emptied out on the back lawn.

The family that owned the home consisted of two parents and three small children; one boy and two little girls. The father worked part time on a ranch not far from his home, but he was paid less than minimum wage because it was classified as farm work and therefore out of the parameters of the Labor Laws. The children played most of the day in their room, quiet as little mice. They never whined to come out, never argued and I never heard the parents get on them.

One afternoon a woman brought me two handmade dolls and told me that she wanted them to go to two little girls. The dolls were "special" and she didn't want them to end up just anywhere. I decided that the easiest way out of this situation was to take them out to the house that we were working on. I hadn't noticed any toys around, so that made my decision even easier.

The next day I arrived with two homemade babies under my arms. I asked Carol, the mother, if the girls would like them and she said that she thought they would. I proudly handed them over, and she took them into the bedroom to give them to the little girls. As she explained to them where the dolls came from I heard Nicholas, the little boy, ask quietly, "What did she bring me?"

I thought my heart would break! How could I have not thought of him, he was a baby. He would not understand this. I decided that I had to return to Cookson to get something for him.

Later that day, I called Nicholas over to me. I took him in my arms and said, "Nicholas, I was thoughtless today. I brought something for your sisters and I didn't think to bring you anything."

Before I could say another word he jumped in and said, "that's okay, I'm just glad my sisters got their babies."

My eyes welled up with tears. I said, "No, honey, I brought you a coloring book. I hope you can forgive me."

"A coloring book!!! Just what I wanted," he cried. "Did you bring me colorings, too?"

I always try to be cognizant when God gives me a life lesson, and this one was coming from a seven year old child. For him to be so selfless and so glad that his sisters received something, even when he didn't, was a big lesson for me. So often I hear about someone else receiving recognition, or getting something special and my response is cynical and selfish. When Nicholas realized that he did get something, he was so excited about it. It was just a coloring book and crayons. It was no big deal, but he was really excited and happy with his coloring book. It is often difficult to appreciate the gifts that God has given to us in this life, especially the smaller ones.

A few days later, Randy and I were sitting on his front porch watching as the work team finished up for the week. Randy turned to me and said, "Meri, you know, I drinks. A whole lot of people come around here and they drinks some, too. I asked my friends, the drunks, if they would help me fix up my house and I couldn't get any of them to help me. I am a full blood Cherokee. I asked Cherokee Nation if they would help me fix up my house and they wouldn't help. I don't even go to church and yet it was the church that came around to help me."

That evening, I sat on my front porch pondering the many times through-out the years that God has placed me in positions with people where my actions and my responses may be the only sermons they ever hear. I pray often that God would make me transparent so that others might see Him through me. I thought of the fine work the teams had been doing on Randy's house, and how much they had helped make this little family's life better. I thanked God for the privilege of standing in the gap between the "haves" and the "have-nots," and for the ability to witness God's presence in the merging of the two.

The following week, we had another team visit. It was going to take at least another week to complete Randy's house. Early Monday morning we loaded up and headed that way for another week of construction.

Randy and Carol had saved their money for three months prior to our arrival so that they could furnish lunch for each group. I noticed that this group didn't seem too enthusiastic about the catfish, beans and cornbread that was fixed for them on Monday. Some ate it and some did not.

After lunch, Carol announced that the next day was Nicholas' birthday and she was going to have cake and ice-cream. Randy leaned over to me and whispered that Nicholas had never had a birthday party and since we were all there, they wanted to give him one.

Tuesday arrived, I picked up a birthday present for Nicholas and we headed for the house. At lunch that day, the group announced that they wanted to go sightseeing in Tulsa and they would be leaving at 1:30. Carol quietly got up and left. You see, they had no freezer, so she needed to travel fifteen miles over dirt roads to town to get the ice cream.

As 1:30 approached the group began to clean up and to pack the tools on the truck. "What about Nicholas' birthday?" I asked. "Carol has gone to get the cake and ice cream,"

"Well, we'll stay for a little while, but we are going to Tulsa," they replied.

At 1:45 Carol had not returned. The group loaded into their car, some sitting on laps because I would not load up my vehicle and return with them. I was staying for ice cream. As they began to close the doors, little Nicholas ran out to the car and asked, "What about my birthday? Mommy's bringing ice cream."

As I watched them drive off, I was reminded that every action, every word that we speak, even every attitude that we carry is testimony to the God (god) we serve. We'd had several occasions to be shinning witnesses for Christ during the weeks that we worked on this house, but this single act of selfishness clouded that witness.

The clear message was that, while they claimed to have traveled to Cookson to "serve the Cherokee People," their own agenda proved to be more important to them than the first birthday party of an eight year old child.

Three witnesses.. .which one was the most powerful?
Which one will you remember?
Which one will Nicholas remember?

SELF STARTERS

I was planning a mission trip for my young people, so I made the drive out to the reservation to talk to their parents. I was sitting in the living room of one of the families where three of my teens lived when suddenly I heard a car start. I looked around and everyone was accounted for. I was always concerned about theft so I jumped up and checked my car. It was fine but the family's car was running.

I told them that someone had started their car and they began to laugh. It seems it had some mal-function and the car would just start by itself. I found that hard to believe and thought they were pulling my leg. Randy went out and turned it off and we went on with our conversation. About twenty minutes later that car started again, Randy went out and shut it off. As I was leaving the car started itself again for the third time that night.

I found myself wishing that we had more Christians who were "self starters". Think how God could use them to further His kingdom.

HOSPITALITY

I loved calling on people on the reservation. It was a wonderful experience to sit in the humble homes of the people and visit and laugh. It didn't matter where I went, there was always coffee and good company at every home. I stopped at an old trailer house one night and we were discussing the fact that the front porch was becoming dangerous.

One of the teenagers came in with a piece of toast. His mother became irritated because he had not offered anyone else a piece of toast. The next thing I know there was a plate of buttered toast in front of me. We began to eat and for some reason that toast really tasted good. We all sat there and ate two loaves of toasted bread.

I felt so guilty about how much I had eaten and I was afraid that the family would not have bread the next day so I went to the market and bought two loaves of bread and delivered them out to the family.

THE GOOD, THE BAD AND THE BEAUTIFUL

Anadarko was a wonderful experience and as my time came to an end I was so grateful for the opportunity to be a part of a Tribe of People so different from my own. I realized that I had learned so much from these wonderful people, so full of life and so open to sharing.

I had about a week left when one of the women missionaries asked me what size shoe I wore. I wasn't sure why she was asking and she finally told me to just put my foot on a paper sack and she traced it off. I dismissed this as peculiar and set about planning my return to seminary. The day I was to leave, I had told the congregation at Wichita that I would leave my name and address on the bulletin board at the church, so I put on my sandals and began the walk over to the church building. As I was walking, I was talking to God and telling Him what a wonderful experience I had enjoyed there on His mission field and how grateful I was that while I had been there for three months, I had not seen a single snake, tarantula, or tornado, and only two scorpions (besides the ones in the storm cellar).

Suddenly, something started to bite me on the top of my foot. I tried to work it out from under my sandal but the more I wiggled around, the harder it bit. I got to the steps of the church and I began to hit my foot on the steps, hoping to get enough pressure to kill whatever it was that was continuing to bite me. I knew that I was going to have to put my finger inside my sandal and dislodge this animal or it would continue to bite. I reached down, dreading what I was going to find and grabbed a sand burr that had worked its way into my shoe. I had a quick vision of God sitting in Heaven and having a good laugh over that one.

I entered the church and was surprised to find all of my new friends there to say good-bye. They had a gift, beautifully wrapped in Indian paper. When I opened it I found the most beautiful pair of moccasins I had ever seen, hand-beaded and custom made to fit my foot alone. I realized why Barbara had wanted me to trace my foot on the paper sack. They are a precious reminder of my time in Anadarko and I still treasure them today.

ANGEL ON THE HILL

The power of suggestion is often very strong and can convince a person of anything.

I believe it was my second year in seminary at Gordon Conwell Theological Seminary in South Hamilton, Massachusetts, that I was studying the different thoughts on the end times. There are those who believe that Christians will be lifted out of this life before the tribulation comes, others believe that Christians will be here for part of the tribulation, and still others who believe that we will experience all of the suffering until the earth is destroyed.

I had been reading articles for each of these three theologies and was steeped in the different philosophies when I walked out of the main building of the seminary. Gordon Conwell overlooked the ocean, though a long way off, and I was trying to catch a glimpse of it when I noticed what looked like an angel on the hill in the distance. It was perfectly shaped and I could even see its head. I listened for the trumpet sound as the hair on my arms stood up. I realized that life as we knew it was about to end...I waited...and I waited...until finally a classmate of mine came out of the building. He saw me watching the hill and asked me what I was looking at. I told him I was wondering what the figure on the hill was and that I had never seen it before.

He looked and told me it was radar for weather detection and that it turned depending on the direction they were watching.

Sure enough, I found myself looking at the hill every time that I went back to campus and the "figure" was always there. Sometimes it looked like a tower, other times it looked like an angel and other times it looked like a big ball on a stand...it all depended on the way you looked at it.

DOES GOD CARE ABOUT A DRESS?

As Easter approached I found myself feeling bad. Easter had always been an occasion in our house when everyone received new clothes. I had never celebrated Easter without a new dress but it was clear that I would not have the money to buy one this year. I remember sitting on the shore of the Atlantic Ocean feeling "left out" because I would not have a new dress and I was apologizing to God for my dilemma. I told God that I simply couldn't afford anything for Easter but if I could I would dress up for Him on that day. I had recently heard that if you want to do something, it is the same to God as doing it. I went home that afternoon and picked up my mail. There in the mail was a check from a friend for $25.00.

Now the guilt set in. I should never have said anything. It was selfish. I decided to give the money to the mission jar at school and let it go overseas and I hoped I would not be this selfish again. The next day I discovered a second check in the mail for $25.00. Again, I was racked with guilt. Why had I made such a big deal out of a dress? Again, I decided to put the money in the mission jar. On Good Friday I went to the mailroom and there was a third check for $25.00.

I told a friend what was happening and he told me that it appeared that God actually wanted me to dress up for Him on Easter. I went that afternoon and found a beautiful dress for $12.00, I bought a pair of shoes for $5.00 and I put the remaining $3.00 in the mission jar. God concerns Himself with every part of our lives if we include Him.

A SPIRITUAL GIANT

My first day on campus was kind of uncomfortable. I didn't know anyone, I had not been to New England before and I was having second thoughts about being there in the first place. I was walking out of the library with an upper-classmate when an older gentleman approached us. He greeted me by name and told me that he hoped I had a good experience there at Gordon Conwell.

As he walked away I looked at him suspiciously, and asked the woman I was with who that man was and how he knew my name. I was told that he was Dr. W. He was a professor there and he knew the names of all the new students. He would go over to the registrant's office in the spring and he would take the applications of the new students, (they all had a picture attached) and he would pray every day for every new student throughout the summer. By fall, he knew everyone.

My undergraduate work was in Physical Education, in other words, I was an athlete, a jock. I taught High School gym and coached for four years before going to seminary. I loved to play any sport and I never lost. The first semester that I was at Gordon Conwell there was a notice posted about a racquetball tournament. I loved racquetball and I signed up immediately. I was a sure winner with all of these scholar-type people. What did they know about racquetball?

The tournament brackets were posted and I had drawn a bye the first round. My first match was to be with Dr. W. "Oh, no! How can I beat that dear little man? He is old, he is frail. This is just not right." For days before the appointed match, I worried, I justified, and I rationalized. This was going to be awful. The whole school would hear about it, I would be known as the woman who destroyed Dr. W.

Finally, the day of the big match arrived. I came to the court dressed in a warm-up suit, Adidas tennis shoes and my personal racquet. I was ready to play. Dr. W. arrived wearing a pair of white shorts, a white t-shirt and deck shoes. My stomach was in my mouth. How could I go through with this? Dr. W. took out his racquet, turned to me and said, softly, "let's have a word of prayer first, Meri." This was just getting worse by the minute. After we had prayed, Dr. W. told me to serve first. "No," I insisted, "you serve first." He finally persuaded me to serve. It was the only time in the match that I touched the ball. He cleaned my clock. I left that court in complete humiliation but I was clearly aware of one thing. Never again would I judge a book by its cover, or a person by their appearance.

THE JOB JAR

Chapel services at Gordon Conwell were required for all students. At ten o'clock every morning, everything on campus closed down, including the coffee shop and the library, as we all made our way to worship together. Preachers came from every corner of the world to share their faith and to inspire us with personal stories and experiences.

The chapel was long and narrow with the pulpit set in the middle, high above the pews. It was simple but elegant. There were no pew cushions and no carpet. The altar area was basic with a communion table and candles. It was seldom decorated. There was an organ and a piano and once a week there was a Praise Band.

One of the finest preachers I have ever heard was this spiritual giant, Dr. W. I've been gone now from seminary for almost three decades, but I can still remember several of his sermons. One cloudy, rainy, morning he was preaching on being a servant. Of course he used the illustration of the washing of the disciples' feet and the words of Jesus to go and be a servant.

Then he told a story about his family growing up. I don't remember how many brothers and sisters he had but there was a family "chore" jar. Every Saturday, before any other activities were engaged, each member of Dr. W.'s family reached into the jar and drew out the two jobs that they would be responsible for in the coming week. By drawing them at random, no one would be stuck with the same job week after week, month after month. As luck would have it, Dr. W.'s. father drew the same two jobs every single time. We all know the old saying, "if it weren't for bad luck, there'd be no luck at all". It seems that for years, Dr. W.'s father was to clean the toilets and wash the dishes.

After the death of his father, Dr. W. and his family had gathered and were reminiscing about family life and how unlikely it was that their father drew the same jobs every week all of those years. It was then that their mother shared how their father had drawn two slips out of the jar and always announced that it was "cleaning toilets and washing dishes" because he knew that those were the two jobs that most people found unpalatable. He did those two jobs to spare his family from having to do something they didn't want to do and he quietly completed the other jobs on the slips that he had drawn from the jar.

What an attitude of servant hood! What a self-less thing to do. So often we are more like Huckleberry Finn, seeking ways to do as little of the unpleasant work as we can get away with and always finding someone else to do it for us if possible. The concept of taking on unpleasant tasks so that others would not have to do them was a novel idea to me. I have remembered it all of these years and I try to follow his example often, especially when I am with a group of people, because I believe that when I follow this man's example, I am following the example of Christ.

"FAITH"

The worship service was over, I was standing at the door shaking hands and wishing people well as they left the sanctuary. A man I had not met stepped up with tears in his eyes and asked if he could speak to me in private. We moved into the corner, and he asked me if I knew of a treatment center he could check himself into to get some help. I told him I could certainly find some people in the congregation to help him, if he wanted them to.

I knew that making a decision to stop drinking and using drugs was generally precipitated by an event, so I asked him what happened.

His eyes welled up with tears again as he told me that he had been arrested for driving under the influence, possession of a controlled substance, and public intoxication. His wife was leaving him and he was sure he would lose his job.

"I know I have a problem with alcohol," he said. "I don't know what to do. I got up this morning and asked God what to do. A friend told me that I should come into this church. When I argued with him, he told me to have a little faith. I really felt out of place at first, but everyone has been so nice. That little girl over there"... he pointed to a four year old who attends Canterbury regularly, "see her? She just gave me this and said she wanted me to have it."

He opened up his hand and there was a very small necklace that simply said "faith".

He looked at me and said, "Now I have a little faith. I know I can get my life back."

CHICKEN OR LOBSTER

I spent the summer between school years in Anadarko, Oklahoma at a mission station there. I had met several people that I dearly loved but there was one in particular, Bertha, who had become a "grandmother" to me. I had invited her to come to New England and spend Thanksgiving with me. She had never been east so she accepted. I rode the train down to the airport to pick her up and we toured around Boston and visited all the attractions while we were there. We went to the shore and watched the fishermen come in with their boats. We went to the docks and watched the lobster traps being brought in.

I asked Bertha if she would like to try lobster and she said, "Yes! I would." I bought several lobsters, but I knew that it was difficult to try new foods; especially if they are as uninviting as a lobster. I told her I would fix a chicken if she weren't sure she would eat the lobster. She insisted when I bought them that it was no problem, she would eat them. She insisted that it was no problem when I put them in a pot and began to cook them. She insisted that it would be no problem when I began to melt the butter. But when I got out the nut crackers she decided that she would have chicken, after all.

Thanksgiving dawned beautifully. The sun was out, it was cold but not too cold and the day promised to be very special, indeed. I had been invited to watch the hunt club go on a hunt that morning and I had never seen one so I got up early that morning and put the turkey in the oven and got everything ready for the feast we were planning. I had Bertha there in New England, I had invited several international students to eat with us, so I viewed this feast to be as close to the original as a person was ever going to get.

The hunt was wonderful. They no longer hunt fox; they take a scented tow sack and drag it behind a horse leaving a trail across many acres of land. Then they turn the dogs loose with the horses right behind them. The riders actually wear black pants, boots, and red jackets with white shirts. I was mesmerized. It was a Thanksgiving to remember.

When we arrived home a short time later, I discovered that the gas had gone out and the turkey was nowhere near cooked. I had guests arriving in an hour and I had a bird that had at least three hours yet to cook. We spent those hours singing, praying, telling stories and laughing. No one seemed concerned that dinner was not served when we had planned it, most of them had never participated in Thanksgiving before so we were simply enjoying being thankful. That was the most memorable Thanksgiving I have ever had.

IS IT WARM?

One of the greatest delights in my life is to be asked to care for someone's children. I love children and I enjoy any opportunity to spend quality time with them. I believe that it is hard to maintain quality time without quantity time and so on those occasions when children stay with me for a week or more I really get involved with them. This week I am taking care of a nine year old boy and his eleven year old sister.

Their father is a single dad and he is a Fire dancer. In the Cherokee Tribe there are men and women who are trained to fight the big forest fires that threaten homes and towns in the spring, when the winds are high and the rains have been sparse. They are famous for going into the high country, or into the roughest terrain to put out fires. When there are fires to fight, they have to be gone for weeks at a time, but the pay is good. When there are no fires, there is no pay and so this family lives very humbly. He was on his way to Arizona and he asked me to keep his children while he was away.

The boy played hard; he had been to the barn, fished at the pond, and collected all of the dirt that a nine year old possibly could on his feet and hands. I told him that he needed to take a shower and get washed up. "I don't really like showers," he told me as I got out a towel, turned on the water and told him where the shampoo was. As I shut the shower door to leave, he looked up at me and asked, "is it warm?"

It doesn't take much to body slam me back into reality! I was suddenly very aware of how much in my life I take for granted. Of course the water would be warm, showers are warm...but not for everybody; many of our children don't know the luxury of regular hot water.

God has given me a very good life and there are too many times when I "expect" the good life and forget to be grateful. I am grateful, today, for the gentle reminder that the advantages that I have are gifts and not everyone has the same quality of life that I have.

WITH A NEW START

As I began my new life and ministry at Cookson, I became acutely aware that anyone working with marginalized people had to include alcoholics and addicts in their ministry. I decided that anyplace as remote as Cookson needed a chapter of Alcoholics Anonymous to meet the needs of those with chemical dependencies.

I attended several meetings in town, eighteen miles away and discovered that there were no meetings on Monday nights. So I decided that Monday night, it was. I made fliers, and announced the beginning of this new meeting everywhere I could. The first night I went over to the main building, made a pot of coffee, drank it and went home. The next Monday evening I went over to the main building, made a pot of coffee, drank it, and went home.

This went on for six months before the first two people arrived for a meeting. Now, before you decide that I am a hero, you must understand that I really like coffee. Attendance at the early meetings varied from two to six but the meetings were always good and we beat the statistics. There were six Charter members of the Cookson 12-Step group. One is still struggling with alcohol and drugs, one died in a car wreck two years after he got sober, and four of us are still in recovery. God changes lives when we allow change.

Through the years, I have watched many people gain control over their chemical addictions with God's help. Sadly, I have watched many more reject God's help and continue to live with the problems of addiction. I have learned one thing, there is no power except God's power and until we decide to turn our will and desire for the chemicals over to God's will and desire for our lives, we will not change. "In John 5, Jesus encounters a man lying by the pool of Bethesda. He says to him, "don't you want to get well?" When the sick man indicates that he does but that there are many excuses for his continued illness, Jesus silences him and says, "Then pick up your pallet and walk."

Chemical Dependency is one of those illnesses that require desire for recovery and I believe that every alcoholic, every addict must answer the question that Jesus asks, "Do you want to get well?" That question must be asked before recovery can begin for many different illnesses and character defects.

CHANGE ME!

Last Sunday, as I was flying home from New York City, I came to realize something about myself. I was getting on the plane in NYC when I noticed a stewardess come from the back and give a strange nod to a second stewardess. She turned to the galley and nodded to a third stewardess. I looked around and there, in first class, was a man with a prayer cap (Jewish), in the next row there was a man of Arab decent, and as I walked further back I observed several other men of Arab decent. I began to get nervous and I almost got off the plane. I haven't felt like that in a long time. I found my seat and sat down, all the time praying, asking God what to do, was this a sign that I should not fly on this plane?

Finally, I decided that there was no basis for my feelings. I asked God to give me a sign that everything was going to be ok. A very young man sat in the seat beside me...he was dark skinned, as was his friend who sat behind me. I began to have thoughts of the "heroes" on 9/11 who had taken on the terrorists in a plane, but had lost their lives when it crashed. I was really getting into it and I prayed again for a sign. It was then that the young man beside me reached down for his backpack...I was ready...and he took out a- Bible. He was a student at Perkins, a Methodist seminary.

Here was the sign. I relaxed and realized that I had a sickness. I judged people based on a single event in history, and on my fear. But when I asked God to help me with this sickness, He provided just what I needed to change. Nothing on that plane changed, all of those people were still there, the stewardesses were still there...what changed was me. I pray that it is permanent.

DOES BEING POOR MAKE ME DIRTY?

I am reminded of a woman who lives on $1,284.00 a year. She is very poor. Her front teeth are missing and she wears ragged clothes. Her hair is often disheveled. One day, she was sitting in my office crying. Her daughter had been arrested and she was left to care for her three grandchildren. She was at wits end and really had no place to turn for help. As we talked, I asked her where God played into her life, whether she had turned any of this over to Him. She hung her head and quietly said to me, "I tried going to church, I been to a lot of them, but them people in the churches make me feel dirty somehow."

ROMANS

It is the custom at Canterbury to invite the children to come forward for a children's sermon. I believe the adults get more out of the children's time than the children do, but we call it a children's sermon just the same. One Sunday in January, around Martin Luther King's birthday, Rick was delivering the children's sermon. He divided the children by eye color, ending up with three different groups. Then he told the children that if they had blue eyes, they could only associate with other children with blue eyes. If they had green eyes, they could not play with children who had brown eyes. He turned to one of our children and told him he could only play with the children in his group. The youngster looked around and discovered he was the only boy. "I don't like girls!" He proclaimed in a loud voice. I want to play with TJ.

"No! TJ has brown eyes, he can't play with you." He was told.

With that, TJ stated in a very loud voice, "WHO CARES?!"

"Who cares?!" What a sermon!

I'M TOO BUSY!

I am acutely aware of the need for grace in my life. Too often everything in my life is about me and my agenda and I find myself stressed and hurried. This leads to tunnel vision and distance from things and people that are around me. Whenever we get tumbling through life, bumping into situations, God in His grace will protect and cushion us. God is always ready to rescue us if we want Him to.

I found myself tumbling and falling one day. Work was extremely busy and people were making demands on my time. I was too busy; my donkey was walking through every fence I put up, I had been gone three weekends in a row, and I hadn't had time to get a sermon ready. My to-do list was growing faster than things were getting done and I had a list of trials and complaints that would stretch from here to NY City. I could go on for hours with all the things that were wrong in my life...and now a child arrived unexpectedly at my house for me to take care of.

Frankly, I was not happy! I was too tired, I was worn out, I was frustrated. I know you won't believe this, but I was CRANKY! In all honesty, I was being very difficult to be around.

I prepared a quick, effortless meal and threw it on the table and we sat down to eat. The child said, "Meri, can I say the grace?" "Please do!" I replied. As we bowed our heads together, I heard this:

"Dear God, Thank you for letting me come here, I am having so much fun! I love it here and thank you for letting Meri love me cause I love her, too. And thank you for this delicious food. Amen. "

Tears streamed down my face. I realized that I had been given a big helping of grace. First, I received grace from the child. She looked past my bad attitude and was grateful for the opportunity that God had given her. And then God had used this child to give His grace to me. No matter how badly I behaved, God had once again gathered me up, placed me back in the nest, and sheltered me with love and grace.

THE FIRE

Wind! The weatherman repeated it over and over. There will be strong winds today gusting at times up to 45mph.

I had gotten up early, but for some reason I just couldn't get moving any faster. I had received three phone calls before 7:30 am. I finally got into the shower and was on my way to work when I noticed a dark cloud of smoke over the trees ahead. "Oh no!" I thought. "It looks like Marlene's house." She is an elderly, handicapped woman and I was afraid that if her house was on fire that she would never get out. As I crested the hill I realized with relief, that the smoke was further down the road. Perhaps it is the church on the corner, or an old garage not far from here. It might even be someone burning tires, but they surely know better with this wind.

As I got a little closer I began to worry that it might be the home of one of the teenagers who had been attending Canterbury Chapel. There were fire engines all over the highway and ambulances with sirens blaring. Instead of turning north toward the Center, I went south to see if there was anything I could do to help.

A small rock house was completely engulfed in flames along with two out buildings and the family car. I pulled up and asked the volunteer fireman who was directing traffic if there was anything I could do. "Pull over there, Meri," he told me. "The family is in that house over there and I think they need someone. He got burned pretty bad."

I went over to the house and found a man sitting on the steps with his arm wrapped in a wet towel, obviously upset. An older woman was standing behind him talking on a portable phone. I introduced myself and asked if there was anything I could do. The woman told me that they were badly shaken and she wasn't thinking very well, but she had left her purse, her glasses, and her prescriptions in the house, and there was nothing left.

I began to explain to them where they could go to get help as soon as they were ready. I told her that we would help her get a new pair of glasses after she had been to the hospital to be checked out. The man looked at me and told me it was all his fault. Their little two year old had set the drapes on fire and he couldn't get them off the wall and outside fast enough. He began to cry as he told me there were several pets in the house that he couldn't get out. He had gotten his mother and his son out but he couldn't do anything for the animals.

As we talked, his wife came running up. She had been called home from work. He tried to explain to her what had happened and she grabbed me and said, "Please! Say a prayer for us." As we sat on the steps of the house next door, I held the hands of these folks and we prayed for comfort, healing and strength for the days ahead.

I stood to leave and noticed that the fire in the house was almost out and the firemen were working on the barn and the garage. There was nothing left, no home, no pets, no car.. .the wind had fanned the flames so that everything was gone in a matter of minutes, leaving this little family with nothing but the clothes on their backs and a prayer.

How quickly life changes. In the twinkling of an eye, everything that we hold as our own, everything that we hold familiar, everything that we hold dear, can be snatched from us. What a hopeless and frightening realization if a person doesn't have prayer to sustain him. Our hope comes from the God who loves us and who gave Himself for us. I can't imagine the desperation of people who do not know this.

HACKY SACK STAYS OVERNIGHT

Holidays always present us with the suggestion of new schedules and added responsibilities. I always plan to put up my Christmas decorations the Saturday after Thanksgiving. I am usually off, so I can get decorating done uninterrupted early in the season and then focus on the many other facets of the ministry at this time of year.

This particular Christmas, Hacky Sacks' mother asked me if he could stay over on Saturday so that they could attend an event of their own. I decided that it would be unwise to put out all of my decorations before his arrival so I left the tree to be done later.

When Hacky Sack arrived and saw my table decorations out, he began to ask me to put up the tree. I told him I was not going to put up the tree this week, but he continued to argue and beg. I held my ground, convincing him that we should go upstairs and watch a movie.

I sat down on the couch beside him and lightly rubbed his back as we focused our attention on "The Lion King." Within the hour he had fallen asleep, so I felt that the problem of putting up my Christmas tree had been solved. I went to bed.

I was awakened suddenly by the beating of a bongo drum. I looked at my clock. It was 2 o'clock in the morning! "HACKY SACK!" I yelled. "Go to bed!" Twenty minutes later I was awakened again. This time I instructed him to come downstairs to sleep on the couch.

Sunday mornings are always an early morning for me. I get up at 4 o'clock and start my day with prayer. I then preach my sermon several times in preparation for the service later that day. The alarm sounded and I got up and made my way to the kitchen to make the coffee. I moved from the kitchen to the living room to check on Hacky Sack, but to my surprise, he was not asleep on the couch. I picked up his blanket to fold it up, and out spilled the salt shaker. Salt was everywhere.

My instincts told me that something was amiss, that I had better go upstairs and find this child to determine why he had taken the salt out. I went up and was confronted with all kinds of problems. The child had gotten into the Christmas closet, taken out the electric train, and painted it with a bottle of white-out he had found in my desk. Decorative balls were scattered around the room. A knick knack I keep on the end of a ten foot beam, eight feet above the living room, was moved to the staircase. He had obviously walked across the beam to retrieve it. There was water in the toy

68

bathtub of my doll house. Several apples and oranges were cut up around the room. Wondering how he had cut, them I searched until I found the butcher knife he had taken from the kitchen.

I was an emotional basket case. How could this child have caused so much damage in such a short time? Why hadn't he slept? How could he have done this to me? And on a Sunday, too!

I woke him up and, with the help of a friend, got him started cleaning up, but it was impossible for me to have any kind of quiet time. It was impossible for me to focus on the day's sermon. It was unthinkable for me to do anything but fret over the damage this child had done in the night when he should have been asleep.

We arrived at church and I spent the morning telling anyone who would listen about the "incident" with this child. I wanted them to commiserate with me. I wanted them to be as incensed as I was. I needed sympathy, I needed support. Rather than focusing on worship, I was totally focused on this gargantuan problem.

Shaken and still angry I entered worship. Hacky Sack was sitting with an adult friend. There would be no further problems from him. As we came to the time in the service for the Pastoral Prayer, I often begin by saying, "I will give you time to pray the prayer that only you can pray," and we enter into a time of silent prayer. As the sanctuary quieted down to pray, the silence was broken by the sound of a child's voice. Hacky Sack began to pray loudly, "Dear God, Thank you for letting me stay at Meri's house last night. I am so sorry that I made her mad. Thank you for her being so nice and forgiving me and I hope you will forgive me, too."

By the time he finished his prayer, there was not a dry eye in the house. The sermon I had prepared did not hold a candle to the one that had just been preached by a five year old child. God often speaks in the most unusual ways.

BE CAREFUL WHAT YOU PREACH!

Eeyore, my donkey, became the terror of the ranch. He chased dogs, armadillos, and cats. He considered it a challenge to go through every fence on the property and when he got out, he would chase cows.

I had a friend who would visit the ranch often. One day she told me that she thought Eeyore had eaten her hat. I knew this hat. It was given to her by her boyfriend and was a very expensive straw hat, with a leather hatband embellished with silver and turquoise conchos. I doubted that Eeyore had taken her hat, and I asked her why she thought Eeyore had "eaten" the hat. She explained to me that the last time she visited, the hat was in the car when she arrived, and when she looked for it later, the hat it was not there.

I knew that her theory was absurd. Did she really think that the donkey had opened the door of the car, taken the hat, and then closed the door again? For weeks I listened to her accusations and denied the possibility that Eeyore could have taken her hat.

One Saturday, as I was walking around the ranch with my young nephew, I noticed an area with what appeared to be scraps of white paper on the ground. "What is that?" I asked, "Let's go pick it up." As we began to gather the scraps, I realized that it was not paper, it was an odd consistency. I really didn't know what it was until Matt picked up the leather hatband. I was flabbergasted! Eeyore must have eaten the hat, after all, but how did he get it? When did he get it?

My pride wouldn't allow me to admit that I was wrong so we gathered up the pieces, put them in a bag, and I put them in my shed. I intended to tell my friend the truth, but I really wanted it to be the at right time and in the right way. "Don't tell Elaine!" I told my nephew. "I will tell her when I am ready. I mean it, don't breathe a word of this to anyone." I believed the matter was settled until I was in a better position to explain.

On Sunday, we all arrived at church. I preached a wonderful sermon on honesty but frankly, I made no connection to the hat. I was going to explain in time. There was NO dishonesty here.

That afternoon, I invited several people to the house for lunch, including my sister's family. I was cleaning up the dishes and since it was such a nice day, the others decided to take a walk. They had walked quite a ways when suddenly my nephew began to cry. He threw his head back and sobbed, "I can't take it anymore! I can't take it anymore!"

Concern mounted as he got more and more dramatic. No one knew what was wrong with this child. Finally, he yelled, "Aunt Meri said God always wants us to tell the truth…Eeyore ate Elaine's hat and Aunt Meri hid it in the shed!"

Everyone was laughing when they got back to the house. They threw open the door, dangled the bag with the remains of the hat and in a chorus of voices yelled, "Be careful what you preach!"

1 Timothy 3:2, "Now the overseer must be above reproach…"

THE WAGON

We have a playground at the Center. We try to keep toys for the children to play with while their mothers are shopping in the thrift store or taking care of their business in the office.

One day I observed two children playing with our wagon in the yard. A little girl was pulling her baby brother around the yard. She had gone around several times and was obviously tiring. She told her brother, "Fred, I'll pull you one more time and then you have to get out." Around they went and when they got back to the gate she said, "There! Now get out."

The baby began to cry and said, "No! no!"

"Ok," she continued, "one more time but then you have to get out"

"Around they went again and when they got back to the gate she said, "OK, get out."

Again the baby cried and said, "No! no!"

Unable to convince her brother to get out of the wagon, she went around again and when she got to the gate she turned to her brother and said, "Fred, we have run out of gas!"

"Run out of gas?" he questioned.

"Yes," she said, "we have run out of gas."

Her little brother got out of the wagon.

"How ingenious!" I thought to myself, and yet, at the same time, how sad that such a young child clearly understands what it means to run out of gas. This is yet another reason why we must never run out of gas in our support of missions.

JESUS IN THE MORNING!

It had been a particularly difficult Sunday with my own services in the morning, caring for two little boys who were spending the summer with me, and now I had to go to a small Indian Church to preach at the evening service and serve communion.

The boys were rowdy on the ride over. I was convinced that they were going to be a problem during the service. I didn't know anyone well enough to ask them to sit with the boys, so I mustered up the strictest face I could and I told them that they were to sit quietly while I preached "OR ELSE!" Both boys looked at me with angelic faces and promised to be good.

As the time came for me to preach, I gave them one last warning look, and went to the podium. I was aware of the boys throughout the sermon, and I was pleasantly surprised at their behavior. They sat relatively quiet for the entire sermon. I blessed the communion elements and invited everyone to "pray in their own way."

The sanctuary became very still as people bowed their heads to pray and then I heard two little voices begin to sing, "Jesus, Jesus, Jesus in the morning, Jesus in the noontime. Jesus, Jesus, Jesus when the sun goes down." Brad looked at me with pride on his face and announced, "We learned that at Bible School, Aunt Meri."

SWEAT PANTS

We have a very small United Methodist Women's group at the Canterbury Chapel, where I pastor. The group decided that they wanted to attend the Jurisdictional Conference because it was going to be in Tulsa and it would not be a long trip for us. We reserved rooms, looked over programs, planned transportation and generally got excited about the weekend with the women from across the Central United States.

The Conference was wonderful and we attended every workshop and activity. Saturday night there was to be a banquet and drama. One of the women of our group had watched as we loaded dress clothes in the van, but she never said anything. On Saturday afternoon, she came to me and told me that she was not going to the banquet, she didn't have anything but sweat pants, and her inability to dress like everyone else embarrassed her.

My first response was to take her to the store and get her something nice, but that would mean missing some of the conference, and I knew it would only further embarrass her. I knew there was nothing I could do, so I accepted her decision. The other women of the group did not, however. When they heard what was going on they got together and decided that they would all wear sweat pants. Being a person in the public eye, I was more than a little concerned about their decision. What if people saw me? What would they think? But I went with it and I was never so proud of a group of women in my life. They all paraded into that banquet hall dressed in sweat pants so that their friend would not be embarrassed.

NICODEMUS

Have you ever had a question that you were afraid to ask because you were afraid of the answer? There are so many times that answers scare us, especially if we think that they might force us to evaluate and make changes in our lives.

These were some of the thoughts that I was trying to pass along in a sermon I was preaching at Canterbury Church one Sunday. We become comfortable in our skin, comfortable with our lives even if they are not what we want them to be or expect them to be. We become comfortable with circumstances, even if they are wrong, because it would be too costly or too risky to change them.

There was a man named Nicodemus who came to Jesus by night. He had questions, he was an honorable man but he wanted assurances that he was going to be saved. Nicodemus. I had used the name Nicodemus several times in the service when one of our little five year olds remarked loudly, "Nicodemus!? My mommy has them patches, too. She ain't going to smoke no more."

Needless to say, the impact of the sermon was slightly diluted but Nicodemus…Nicoderm? Both are about taking risks, giving up things, and changing to become better people.

THE CROSS

There is a conference center just North of Birmingham that I've had the opportunity to visit on several occasions. It sits in a hollow, majestic hills surround it. It is remote and really beautiful.

The lodge has a porch encircling the building, furnished with rocking chairs. The first time I was there, I was sitting out on the porch with a group of people late one night. We were talking and enjoying the mild weather, when one of us noticed a cross up on the hill across the hollow. It was a large cross and was lit up for everyone to see. We began to talk about this cross and decided that we would ask if there were a trail up to it that we could climb the next day.

I went to the camp manager and asked him about the possibility of climbing up to see the cross on the hill. He told me that there was a trail right to the cross, but if we decided to go, we needed to look him up and get a key. I was puzzled, why would we need a key?

The manager explained to me that the camp had been forced to put a fence around the cross because **there had been a lot of people who had gone up to the cross who didn't belong there.**

A lot of people who had gone to the cross who didn't belong there? Those words stuck in my head, and all day long I thought about them. People going to the cross who don't belong there. I thought of Canterbury Chapel and of all the people who have attended over the years. People who have needed the cross, people who have needed a Savior, and each one feeling at some time or another that they didn't belong there, but each life changed when they finally encounter the cross.

I was forced to ask myself how many times I had put a fence around the cross. What made me think I had the right to decide who could come to the cross and who could not. I do know this, everyone belongs at the cross. Everyone who manages to get to the cross, everyone who discovers the love and forgiveness of the cross, has a life changing experience. After all, isn't that what the cross stands for?

JUST JUMP RIGHT IN

Summer in Oklahoma is intensely hot. It is not uncommon to have 30 to 35 days in a row of temperatures over 100° with high humidity. There is no escape. There is nothing one can do to change it, so we are left with the challenge of finding ways to deal with it. Of course, there is air conditioning, but that means staying indoors all of the time. Most people find some comfort in swimming, and have a favorite place where they can submerge themselves in cool water to escape the torture of the heat.

I hadn't been in Oklahoma very long before I saw the practicality of owning a pool. Not a large one, just an above-ground pool where I could relax, float, get wet and attempt to endure the three months of the year that are so intense.

I seldom went into the pool alone. There was always someone who was interested in swimming with me. Going to the pool was a "family affair" everyone who was swimming, and often those who were not including the dogs, the horses, and the donkey made the trek down the hill with humans carrying towels, flip flops, and a cold glass of tea or pop.

It was a hot, lazy day and we intended to spend the day at the pool. I was floating on a raft, just enjoying the serenity around me. Duke, my energetic golden retriever, was sleeping in the driveway at the top of the hill. We had been swimming for about an hour and Elsie decided that she wanted to get some sun. She climbed the ladder, gathered up her towel and her suntan lotion, and headed for the chaise lounge. I watched, disinterested, as she spread her towel out on the plastic chair and covered herself with lotion. It took her several minutes to figure out how to get the chair to lie flat so that she could lie on her stomach and tan her back.

As I drifted dreamily around the pool, a movement at the top of the driveway caught my attention. Duke was awake and watching the process. His ears went up and he cocked his head to the side. As Elsie climbed into the lounge, Duke stood up.

"Watch Duke," I quietly instructed the others who were in the pool. We gathered at the side of the pool and watched as Elsie settled into restful repose. Duke, seeing that she was lying down and at his level, began to run directly at the chaise lounge. He never slowed down as he jumped over Elsie's head and landed in the middle of her back. Elsie screamed. The legs of the chaise lounge gave way, dumping her and Duke to the ground. It didn't phase Duke one bit. He was so excited to have someone close enough to him that might love on him that he squirmed and rolled, then settled down in the middle of her back and proceeded to lick off all of her lotion.

As I watched Duke pursue the opportunity for companionship, I couldn't help but relate this circumstance to church. There are so many times that new people come to the church, enthusiastic and energetic. They want fellowship, they want to be a part of something. They want to contribute, but they are often given a less than enthusiastic response. New ideas are countered with well known responses, "We've never done it that way before", or "We tried that, it didn't work." Enthusiasm is squelched with cynicism or suspicion. Ownership and territorialism tear away at creativity, and before long new ideas are either kept unspoken or the newcomer simply leaves.

The church can do better. We must develop attitudes that embrace the energetic and enthusiastic. We must seek ways to channel new energy, to give life-flow to its creativity. It is imperative. The future of the church depends upon it.

"THAT'S MY CHURCH"

He came to church the first few times with the court-ordered treatment center. They attended our services two or three times a month. He never said a word to anyone and headed out to the van as soon as church was over.

When he started coming to church on his own, none of us could believe it. He was so beaten by drugs and alcohol that it was going to be a long climb back. His body was in terrible shape. He had lost his business, been in jail, his wife left him, and he had no transportation. He was forced to move in with his mother.

Several months went by and we witnessed a miraculous transformation; he got a job, his health came back, he was working a program and not drinking or using. One Sunday he surprised us by bringing his mother. She didn't say much, but I shook her hand at the end of the service. The next week she was there, and she brought her mother. They attended faithfully, but never really seemed to get involved except when we had potluck. Both women loved to cook and they were wonderful at it. We began to look forward to whatever they brought.

One day, I ran into the mother in the grocery store. She was fuming! She walked right up and began telling me why she was so mad. It seems that a friend of hers, from the church she had attended before she started coming to Canterbury, had approached her in the grocery store and told her that her church missed her.

"Well," mother replied, "I am going to another church, now."

"Where?" Her friend asked.

"Canterbury Chapel," she responded proudly.

"Why, that's where all the drunks go!" she told her. "You don't want to be associated with that kind of people!"

"Let me tell you something," the mother said hotly. "That's my church! There are people going there that would never come to church if it hadn't been for them. They are my friends. Maybe if the church had a few more "drunks" *in* it, there would be a few less drunks out there suffering. I think that is important!" With that, she turned and stomped away.

It was at this point that I ran into her.

"When," she asked, "did the church become a place that only perfect people could go? When *did* the church become a place that didn't want to be associated with certain kinds of people?"

I had no answer for her. I still don't. As I read the Gospels, I am unable to find anyone that Jesus refused to be associated with. When did the church become such an elite place?

GOD WANTS ME TO DO WHAT?

"Hello? This is Meri." I answered the phone hesitantly. I was at the office when my Administrative Assistant announced that the Bishop was on the phone. Now, for those who are not Methodist, when the Bishop calls, he always gets my attention. I wondered what he wanted with me.

"Meri," he said, "I need you to do me a favor."

When the Bishop says he needs a favor, it is clear to me that it is not always a request, so I asked, "What can I do for you, Bishop?"

"Meri, there is an Oklahoma Indian Missionary Conference Church down in your area called Canterbury Chapel. Last week the Pastor that I had appointed there resigned and moved out. The congregation has informed me that they will not be returning, either. I need you to go down there and keep the doors open until I can find another pastor."

I had been to Canterbury once, so I knew where it was. After reviewing my calendar, I told the Bishop that I could fill the pulpit for a few weeks until he found someone else.

It was August. August in Oklahoma can be brutally hot. Sunday arrived and I packed up a carefully scripted sermon and headed for the Church, not knowing what the congregation had been told or what to expect. I arrived at the church in plenty of time to meet people and find out what kind of service they were used to. No one was there. In Indian country, there is a thing called "Indian time," which means; whenever people assemble and are ready. So I waited. I did not have a key, so I sat in the hot car for an hour and thirty minutes. True to their word, the congregation did not show up. I went home.

The next Sunday I arrived at the church a little closer to worship time. I had the same sermon I had prepared the week before. I hadn't used it so there was no need to write another one. I sat in the parking lot for an hour before going home.

The third Sunday two people showed up and I finally got to preach that sermon. For over a year the congregation consisted of those two people and any of my friends or family that I could beg to come. Every time I managed to get someone to try the church, they were met with an attitude of owner-ship.

As Annual Conference approached and the time came to appoint pastors to their churches, my phone rang again. It was the District Superintendent.

"Meri," he said, "you are going to take Canterbury Chapel again, aren't you?"

"No, David, I'm not." I answered. "I'm tired of preaching to two people."

"But you have to," he pleaded. "You know I can't afford to send a pastor down there."

"David," I informed him, "that church is suicidal. It is killing itself. You need to just let it die."

"Oh," he said, "we don't do things like that in the Methodist Church."

"David, the church is dead." I continued. "It can't be resurrected. You need to just bury it."

"We just don't do things like that in the Methodist Church, Meri. I'll tell you what. You pray about it and get back to me." He said.

"David, please. I'm a pastor, I've already prayed about it. God told me He didn't want me to go down there anymore." I informed him.

"Meri, I am a District Superintendent. God told me He did."

Not knowing how to respond to that line of reasoning, I agreed to pray about it for a week, but I knew I was not going to change my mind. Later that week I was traveling to a United Methodist Women's meeting in Western Oklahoma. I had said I would pray about the Church, so I did. As I was lamenting my decision to God, I began to think about all of the Alcoholics Anonymous and Narcotics Anonymous Meetings I had attended.

When you enter an AA meeting, no one cares what you have done. No one cares how you are dressed, how you talk, whether you have ever been in prison, whether you smoke, what color your skin is or how much you can put into the collection basket. They are just really glad you are there. I began to wish that the church could go to an AA meeting and see how that is done. Then it occurred to me that I seldom see members of AA or NA at any church, and God began to work on my desires.

I went home and called the District Superintendent. I told him I would take the church again on one condition, that he allow me to make it a 12-Step Church for people in alcohol and drug recovery.

"You do whatever it takes to keep the doors open," he told me. I knew he didn't know what he had just agreed to.

It didn't take long before I regretted my decision to keep the church. I was tired, I was discouraged, and I didn't want that commitment every week. As

I gathered a few recovering alcoholics to help me plan this new ministry, I began to subtly sabotage it. It was decided that we would start off with a bang and open the doors on the Fourth of July. I knew that everyone would be at the lake and have no interest in attending church. We would fall flat on our faces and we would be able to say, "Well, we tried. Nobody came."

The Fourth of July arrived. It was hot! I stood in the pulpit arranging my notes for the day's sermon. I was angry that I had buckled under the pressure to take the church. I was sure that nothing had changed and now I would struggle with a new problem. As I stood there fuming, I became aware of a noise out on the street. The north side of the sanctuary was lined with windows and I looked up to see four motorcycles coming down the street and park in the church parking lot. Seated on those four motorcycles were four men.

They wore black leather pants, black leather vests, boots, chains, long hair, tattoos and earrings. Riding behind them on those motorcycles were four women. They wore black leather pants, black leather vests, boots, chains, long hair, tattoos and earrings. They sat on the south side of the sanctuary and listened intently as I preached. There were twenty seven people in the service that day.

At the close of the service, one of the men raised his hand and asked whether I would allow him to say something. He stood quietly at his pew for several minutes. I was just about ready to go on when he looked at me and said, "Mama, I've been in prison for fifteen years. Damn! I didn't think I'd ever go to church, and I sure as hell never thought there would ever be a church that would have me. But I needed this!"

For those of you who find yourselves more concerned that a man cussed in the worship service that day than you are that there are people who feel the church won't have them, I'm here to tell you that your priorities are all messed up!

Through the years, I have learned that sometimes when I get messages from God, I can create them to be exactly what I want God to say. It is important to be open to God's leading through other people as well. My resistance to keeping the church open would have deprived me of the opportunity to watch God change, rehabilitate, redeem, and restore life to hundreds of people. People that the rest of the world often avoid or ignore. People that the rest of the world often fear. The kind of people that Jesus often found himself having dinner with. What a blessing!

Canterbury Chapel has grown through the dedication of people who claim that they have already been to hell and they don't want to go back there. They have had to build a new sanctuary because they outgrew the old one. They have a strong youth program, a strong mission program, they have had five members declare candidacy for the ministry and they have become a safe haven in the chemical dependency community.

"I sure as hell never thought that I would ever find a church that would have me."

CHAPTER FOUR

"A joyful heart is good medicine…"

PROVERBS 17:22

NAILED!

Many of the groups that come during the summer to work are youth groups. Most of the youth are very energetic and anxious to make a difference while they are there, but there are always those who have a knack for getting into trouble.

I was greeting a new group one evening, getting them settled into the lodge when a young man came up to me and asked me if I was in charge. Having no one else around to point at, I had to admit that I was in charge.

"Well," he told me, "we have 'girls' in our group."

"Ok?" I questioned, wondering what he was getting at.

"Girls." He repeated and looked at me as if I were entirely missing the point.

"Ok." I repeated still unable to make a connection.

"Girls don't know how to build anything," he stated. "They will just slow us down. I think that they should stay here and fix our meals, or clean, or help around the office."

"Well," I exclaimed, wondering how he had missed the fact that I was also a 'girl'. "We are not gender specific here." I could tell by the look on his face that he had no idea what I meant. "I think that we will take them with us anyway and just see what happens."

Now, when you are working with teens, girls are better roofers than boys. When you are putting on shingles they have to go down very straight. There is one way to do it and the roofer must pay special attention to every shingle or the entire roof will be off. *Girls will do exactly what you tell them to do, the way you tell them to do it.* It may take them all day, but those shingles will be straight.

Boys, on the other hand, want to know if they can drive the nail in three hits, two, or one hit. They compete to see who can put down the most shingles in the least amount of time.

We were working on a trailer house that needed a bedroom added on. There were five children in the family and the trailer was a two bedroom. We were also putting a roof over the top. I told my foreman to take the boys out front and begin framing the room and I would take the girls up to the roof and begin shingling.

The worrisome young man informed me that I didn't want to do that! I gathered up my tool belt and hammer and started up the ladder. I always work the edge so that everything gets started straight. I gave instructions to the girls and we started. Nothing would do but that the young man sat down beside me. He was roofing with both feet out behind him in a posture that was almost anatomically impossible. As we worked, he would look down the line and ask me, if I thought the girls were putting the shingles on straight? Had I seen how one of the girls had driven that nail? Did I notice how many hits it took the other one to drive the nail?

Finally, I nailed his pants to the roof and called "lunch." I had to explain to him that some unknowing "girl" probably had nailed his pants to the roof accidentally.

The next summer I was waiting to greet a new group and to get them settled in the lodge. A very tall young man came up to me and asked me if I remembered him. I told him that I was afraid not and he told me that I had nailed his pants to the roof the summer before. He never said one derogatory word about 'girls' that summer.

The next summer I received a letter from a young man who started out with "You may not remember me, but you nailed my pants to the roof." He went on to say that he had decided to become a missionary himself and wanted to come to Cookson for the entire summer as a volunteer.

We never know how God will use a person's experience in the mission field, but we must always be ready for a miracle, even if it seems really unlikely.

YANKEES

Groups who came to work from the North and the East were lovingly called "Yankees". We always showed extra concern when a Yankee group was to visit because they were so unaware of many of the "critters" that we have in Oklahoma that can be dangerous.

For example, you can always tell a Yankee group if you drive up at lunch time and everyone is sitting in the grass. We have these irritating little bugs called chiggers that will "eat you alive" once they get into your skin.

It was Spring Break and we had a group of Girl Scouts coming to work on their Gold Award. They were given the responsibility of roofing a small house south of Cookson. April is a very pleasant time of the year for us, but we are still wearing blue jeans and sweatshirts. The girls came out of the lodge wearing shorts and tank tops. They insisted that they were going back to school with a tan since they had traveled all the way to Oklahoma.

We climbed up on the roof and began to work. After two hours, I called for a break and climbed down the ladder, but when I turned around, all of the girls were lying "spread eagle" on the roof. I got a drink, rested a few minutes and went back to work. Every time I would announce a break they would all lie down on the roof, soaking up the rays.

After the third day, I decided that these girls were not coming down off the roof for a break, so I took the water up on the roof. As I was sitting on the ridge, the advisor suddenly sat up and said, "Look girls, there's a hawk up there circling. That's a good sign, isn't it Meri?"

"Well, yes, it is a good sign if a hawk is circling overhead," I responded.

"Look! There's another one. Oh! This is so great! ANOTHER ONE! I can't believe it there are three…no four! This is so great, isn't this great, Meri?"

I looked at her and said, "Y'all better start moving around, the buzzards are starting to circle." I'm not sure that she has ever believed that those were buzzards not hawks.   Yankees!

WHY I BECAME A UNITED METHODIST

I was ordained an American Baptist Minister when I graduated from seminary and went to serve a large church in Lockport, New York. I was to be the Director of Christian Education and Missions. The first year that I was there was an ideal time, the youth group was active, the programs were going very well and everyone seemed to be responding to the leadership of the church.

One day the Senior Pastor called me into his office and told me that there were several people in the church who had indicated an interest in being baptized and so there would be a baptismal the following Sunday evening. He also told me that there were some of the youth who wanted to be baptized, too, and since I had been working with them, he felt that I should baptize them. I thanked him and left the office.

I felt very uneasy about the upcoming baptism because I did not know how to baptize anyone. I had a friend who was a student at Colgate Rochester Divinity School and was also an American Baptist, so I asked her if she knew how to baptize. She looked at me with a puzzled look on her face and said "no".

We decided that we should go to the church and practice so I called the Chairman of the Board of Deacons and asked him when the baptismal would be filled. He told me that they filled it by Thursday but it wouldn't be warm until Saturday. We decided that we would go to the church late Saturday night when no one was around and practice.

At ten o'clock on a Saturday night in January, we put on our shorts, tee shirts and our winter coats and headed to the church. We didn't want anyone to know that these two clergy women did not know how to baptize so we only turned on the light above the baptismal. That way if anyone was driving by they wouldn't see the lights and be tempted to come in and see what was going on.

The sanctuary was cold as we took off our coats and stepped into the pool. If you are not Baptist, you may not know that at the bottom of a baptismal there are slat boards to keep you from slipping and to keep the drain free. Once we were settled in the water we began to discuss what we needed to say and how we were going to go about this baptism. I glanced down and there, swimming out from under the slat boards was a long thin "wiggly" thing. It swam right in front of us sending us into a panic as we fought for the lead position getting out of the water. We got up on the top step and turned to look into the water and my friend asked, "Is that a leech?"

"I think so," I replied as we watched this creature swim across the pool and begin to surface on the other side. All I could think of was that it took three days to fill the pool, three days to heat the pool and there were probably a hundred more under that platform. How would they ever get them out before the service tomorrow night and how would I know that they were out?

As the "leech" swam to the other side it kind of flopped over on its side so that we could get a better look at it....it was a palm frond left over from Palm Sunday.

Sunday evening arrived and the mood was set in the church. The lights were dim, the organ was playing softly in the background and there was a child dressed in a robe with a big bow tie who was to light a candle every time someone was baptized.

The Senior Pastor had already baptized three people when it was my turn to perform my first baptism. The young lady that was first on my list weighed in at 260 pounds. We had spent the afternoon discussing how she would go with me; just let her knees go, duck under the water, and then stand back up. We had practiced, it was time. I said some things about the act of turning your life over to God and then I said, "in the name of the Father, and of the Son and of the Holy Spirit." As I went to help her under the water, she literally dove backwards right out of my hands. When she hit the water and started down, she splashed water over the front of the pool and onto the altar, putting out three candles. I looked down and the little "cherub" was holding up her hands and shaking her head as if to ask, "now what?'.

I rushed over to where my convert was splashing and sputtering and I grabbed her and tried to pick her up. She had a little white hankie that I was supposed to use to wipe her face and I grabbed it and held it over her mouth so that the congregation did not know what had happened. As the water settled and we got out of the pool the Senior Pastor began his decent with this young ladies' mother.

She was as big as her daughter, but she was afraid of the water. As the Pastor went to dunk her under the water she reached up and grabbed the front of the baptismal and held on, so the Pastor put his knee on her chest and pushed her under.

As I stood on the landing and watched this I thought to myself, "there has to be an easier way to do this!" So when I was offered the opportunity to become a United Methodist, ...I grabbed it!

COWBOYS AND INDIANS

My nephews were visiting me from New York: tickets to the rodeo were a must. They loved to watch all of the events but they were especially fond of bull riding. When the music would start that precluded the bull riding, the boys would go down in front of the bleachers and begin "riding." One of them would play like he was on the bull, with a little hand in the air, while the other one doubled as announcer and gate tender. They would say in a very loud voice, "He's dwan him a wank bull here tonight wadies and gentlemen…the daddy wabbit. Slides up on dat bull, nods his head and he calls for it." By this time they had the attention of everyone in the stadium as the gate keeper would pull the imaginary rope to turn the bull out and the other one came out twisting and bucking until the buzzer either sounded or he got thrown off.

I decided since they were so intrigued by bull riding, I would hang a barrel bull at my place for them to play on. My friend Charlie came to help me get it hung just right in the trees. In an effort to impress the boys I told them, "Charlie used to ride bulls. In fact, Charlie was a cowboy just like the ones in the rodeo."

The older of the two boys looked up with a confused expression and said, "I thought Charlie was a Indian."

BIG MENS

My nieces had all spent the night recently and we called it "girls' night." TJ lamented the fact that he could not go to "girls' night," so I promised him that we would have "boy's night." Well, it didn't happen in a reasonable amount of time and I knew that I had to do something soon or he would become discouraged. I stopped by his house one night to ask if I could take him to a local restaurant for a burger. His mother teased him, asking how it could be "boy's night" when Aunt Meri was not a boy. I simply told him that he was a boy and that made it all right.

We arrived at the restaurant and he told me all about his day at school. Then he realized that the walls were decorated with hunting trophies of all kinds; there were deer, and buffalo, fox skins and snake skins. With this came all of the questions; who killed them, how did they die, why did they kill them and so on. Finally, about halfway through our meal, he put his elbows up on the table and said to me, "I love this, Aunt Meri! 'Cause this is what us big mens' like to do, ain't it?"

WHO'S A GENTLEMAN?

We try to instill in our children many of the social mores that are required as they move through life. The supervisor of our children's program had worked all year on the concept of boys being gentlemen. He would make the boys wait until the girls were served lunch, and then they could get into line. He would say to them, "That's the gentleman thing to do." He would make them help the girls get in the van to go home, and then he would say to them, "That's the gentleman thing to do."

One hot summer day I was asked to officiate a funeral in the area. My customary dress at work is a pair of blue jeans and a t-shirt, or if I am working on the Volunteer In Mission Team, I will wear bib overalls. This particular day I had my hair up and I was wearing a dress. I went to the gym to check on the children's program. As I entered the doorway two young boys were walking past me.

One of them stopped, looked up at me and said, "You look beautiful today, Miss Meri".

I was extremely flattered and said, "Thank you, honey. That's the nicest thing anyone has said to me in a long time."

The boys walked on past and I heard my admirer say to his friend, "That's the gentleman thing to do."

DIFFICULITIES

I was hot! There were two girls at my house playing in the pool, performing all sorts of cheerleading and water ballet maneuvers. It was apparent that they didn't know what they were doing, but they really wanted to. The younger one yelled for me to watch her as she attempted to do a back flip in the water. She tried once, then again. I gave her some tips on how to turn under the water and she tried again, and then again. Finally, she came up coughing and sputtering and said, "I can't do this, my brain floats too much."

SOOOO TIRED

I was responsible for the children's after school program at church for a while, so I made arrangements for us to go to a neighboring church to use their gym twice a week. The other church was about four blocks from ours and we simply bundled up the children and walked over. It was a cold night as we walked and the wind was blowing. We were all in a hurry to get where it was warm, but we had one straggler in the group. I encouraged him to go faster, I pushed him, I waited on him, and I hurried him. Finally, in frustration, he sank down in a snow bank and looked at me with a sad little face and said, "Meri! My feet are out of breath."

ONE NOSE

I love to engage children in conversation and to challenge them in the knowledge that they believe themselves to have. On one such occasion I asked a three year old, "Do you know how to count?"

"Yep!" Came the reply.

"OK then," I went on, "how many eyes do you have?"

"Two," he responded.

"How many ears do you have?"

"Two," he said.

"How many hands do you have?"

"Two."

"How many feet do you have?"

"Two."

"How many lips do you have?"

"Two."

To each of these responses I replied, "GOOD!" Then I asked, "How many noses do you have?" He caught himself just before he said two, and thought a minute. "One"! He replied proudly.

"How come, if you have two of everything else, you only have one nose?" I continued.

He thought for a minute and then he said, "Well, lots of people got only one nose."

GHOST BUSTERS

I attended a revival one evening with some of our more enthusiastic brethren in the faith. The preacher was a young father and he brought his three young sons with him.

These boys were dressed in little suits and ties and sat on the front row, perfect little gentlemen as their Daddy preached from the front. As the service was drawing to a close the preacher began the usual altar call… "With every head bowed, every eye closed…," he began with fervor. The intensity of the "call" increased as he sought commitment from the congregation. "Lord," he began to shout, "send your Holy Spirit into this place. We ask you Father, touch our souls with your Holy Ghost, send your **Holy Ghost into our midst!!!**"

It was at this point that a small voice from the front row was heard to sing, "Who ya gonna call? Ghost Busters! Who ya gonna call? Ghost Busters!"

Needless to say the revival ended at that point.

WHAT HAPPENED

Early in my ministry I had the opportunity to go to northeastern Arizona to work on the Hopi and Navaho Reservations. Summer always brought the prospect of Vacation Bible School and we would gather fifty to one hundred excited children and treat them to songs, stories, crafts, games, and snacks.

One rather warm morning we had assembled the children for opening exercises and singing. I had my guitar and we had sung several songs and were preparing for a puppet show. A little girl, about five years old was sitting beside me. She was fascinated by my guitar and was quietly strumming the strings while we waited. When the puppet show began, I just put my hand over the strings so that they wouldn't play. The child looked up at me inquisitively and asked, "What happened? Run out'ta batteries?"

CAN'T SAY THAT

One morning I was caring for a two year old in my home. He was riding a tricycle in the driveway and I was working around in the house. I would check on him periodically to be sure that he was staying where he was supposed to. Suddenly, the peacefulness of the country was interrupted by the child's piercing screams. I ran from the house expecting to find him sprawled out on the driveway, spurting blood everywhere, or bitten by a snake, or some other unimaginable disaster.

As I approached him he was holding his mouth. I envisioned all of his teeth knocked out, or serious damage to his tongue, but I saw nothing.

"What's wrong?" I asked desperately.

The child pointed to his mouth. I discovered, upon closer inspection, that he had picked up a fuzzy caterpillar and put it in his mouth. It was wiggling and he didn't know what to do.

"Well, spit it out," I told him.

He spit the confused little critter out on the ground and bent over to look at it.

"Do you know what that is?" I asked him.

He looked up at me, tears still running down his face, and replied,

"A pillicopter!"

CHAPTER FIVE

"O my people, hear my teaching; listen to the words of my mouth. I will open my mouth in parables, I will utter hidden things, things from old-"

PSALM 78:1-2

AIRPORTS AND PEOPLE

This past weekend, I was traveling to New York City and I had a layover in Dallas. As I rushed to my gate, it was suspiciously quiet and there were very few people sitting in the waiting area. I went up to the desk and asked if the plane to New York had already boarded. The attendant told me that the gate had been changed. I took off at a run, although I was sure I still had plenty of time to catch my flight. As I arrived at the gate that was now to be the location of my flight, I saw a woman sitting off by herself. "Are you going to LaGuardia?" I asked. She told me no, that she had just sat down there for a few minutes.

I was intrigued because everyone else was hustling around to their respective gates so I asked her where she was going and she began to cry. She told me that her mother had died unexpectedly and she was on her way to Washington to the funeral. She was to meet her sister in about an hour and she had just sat down there to wait for her. We began to talk and I shared with her that I believed that her mother was in a better place and that she could believe that she would see her again. I hugged her as they called my plane and as I left she told me, "I didn't know why I sat here, I could have picked any gate in the airport…thanks."

I walked away knowing both why she sat where she did and why my gate was unexpectedly changed. Thank you God! Amen

HOW GOD IS WORKING IN THE DAY CARE

The new building was to house a Senior Citizen's Nutrition Center and a daycare. The Senior's program was up and running with record breaking attendance. It was time to focus on the day care. I contacted an agency in town, fully expecting them to be delighted with the idea of putting a day care in our new building. We had several meetings but there just wasn't any progress. November came and it was time to think about Christmas. We needed to focus on applications, receiving gifts, and setting up. Daycare was put on hold.

After Christmas, I left for a three month sabbatical, so we continued the hold on daycare. When I returned, I decided that it was time that "I" do something about this so I began to court this agency again. There was still no progress. I wrote and gave them a deadline which they didn't meet. Now it was time to pray.

"Lord," I prayed, "what are we supposed to do? Where are we going to find people who are interested in developing a daycare program? I don't have time to pursue avenues for licensing or furnishing a day care. I don't want to be responsible for staffing and running a daycare. What do I do? Where do I turn?"

Almost immediately the name of a friend came to me. She already had a daycare in a neighboring town, but I thought that maybe she would like to expand, or maybe she knew someone she could refer us to. I told her what I was looking for and she said she would pray about it. Three days later she called to say that she and her husband had talked about it, and she would take on our day care, also.

The very next day a woman walked into my office and asked to speak to me. She had just moved to the lake and wanted to do some volunteer work for us. I asked her what she did for a living. She informed me that she wrote grants for Head Start and daycare centers. I sat, stunned, as we discussed the needs for the day care and how to go about getting started. She began writing grants immediately and getting in touch with resources she was acquainted with. Within the week, she was introduced to the day care director and they began to plan and dream together.

It is customary for us to begin every week with a staff meeting and a prayer. It had been just two weeks since the wheels were set into motion for the daycare. We were just settling down to pray, when the front door flew open and in walked two women and a man. I got up and went to tell them that we didn't open until 9:00 am. They would need to wait another fifteen minutes before we could serve them.

The man was the spokesperson. He wanted to know who was in charge I told him I was, and that we still didn't open until 9:00. He was not to be deterred. "We are here to volunteer," he said.

That got my attention! I invited them to come in and pray with us. When the prayer was over, I began to ask questions about this unusual offer. They wanted me to show them around the Center and explain what we did, so we walked and talked.

They were from Western Pennsylvania. They were a part of a Christian Community there and the community had decided that it needed to be more involved with other Christian efforts across the country. This community had purchased bus tickets for eighty constituents, given each one $50.00, and directed them to go into the world and make a difference. They were to volunteer to do anything that they were asked to do, and take no pay for it. They were to stay as long as they could find housing and felt that they were truly making a difference.

Assuming that they were farmers, I asked them what they did to make a living in Pennsylvania. The wife and mother spoke up. They built furniture for daycare centers. I asked them if they could build us a few pieces and they agreed. After three weeks, they came into my office and announced that we needed to talk. Assuming that they were ready to return home, I invited them to come in and sit down.

"We have been on the phone with our community back home and they said that if you would bring a truck and come to Pennsylvania, they would fill it with everything that you need for your daycare."

When God is consulted about our ministries, we can only sit back in awe and watch His work. For three people, who aren't even Methodist, to come all the way from Pennsylvania to a place called Cookson, Oklahoma to build daycare furniture for our children at the very time that we needed it is a thrill that only comes from a loving Father. Thank you so much God for this witness.

CAN'T WE ALL BE GRATEFUL?

A couple of months ago, I was at the home of a friend of Cookson. His floor was caving in, his roof leaked, he had no car, and he is 87 years old. Each summer, he raises a huge garden and his wife either cans or freezes everything that comes out of it. I asked him about that garden. I asked him why he raised such a large garden at his age.

He turned to me and said, "Meri, when our check comes at the first of the month, I go into town and pay my bills, electric, water, taxes and the doctor. I pay for a ride to town. When I get done, I have seven, maybe eight dollars left for the month. If I didn't raise that garden, we wouldn't eat." Then he added, "I'm just thankful to God that I can still work a garden."

I was humbled. Here was a man full of thanks when he could have been resentful. Here was a man grateful for what he had, not frustrated with what he didn't have. Here was a man full of Thanks!

THE GARDEN

There was a low area on the property at Cookson. We often discussed the fact that the 1/2 acre area was a waste because it was so wet and "snaky". No one wanted to go out there for fear of coming across one of the many water moccasins that lived there. A wonderful friend of the Center had given us a green house and I was standing out in the field discussing the new location of the greenhouse in relationship to the other visions that we had for the Center.

We were still in need of a playground, we wanted to put in a volleyball court, we needed parking. I looked at that swampy area and said to myself, "I wish we could haul in some gravel, build that area up and put the greenhouse out there." My imagination began to get carried away. I saw the greenhouse with water and heat. I saw raised garden beds with walkways in between and maybe even some garden benches. We would involve the senior citizen's and pick on the halves.....

Later that day I was delivering a meal to one of our shut-ins. I invited two of our volunteers to go with me, a retired couple from Arkansas who had stopped to visit on their way out west. We were carrying on a conversation and I was telling them my ideas about the greenhouse and the garden.

"Why, you don't need to go to all of that expense," they told me, "We are retired farmers from southeastern Arkansas. We farmed below sea level and were always standing in water. You can build levies and that water will run right off."

When we returned to the Center, later that day, we walked out and looked at the field. "This would be great for blackberries and muscadines (a grape-like fruit)," they told me. "Then you could make jelly and sell it."

It just so happened that I was to speak in the area they were from just one week later. I invited them to make this wasteland a special project and they agreed. They have built levies, plowed the field, purchased and planted blackberries and muscadines, set up the greenhouse, and helped to build a small building that we use for a fruit stand. They return four times a year to prune and weed the beds. We use the fruit to make jellies and jams we sell to support the Senior Citizen's Program.

Churches often take trips to Cookson to see firsthand what we are doing. On one such tour, I was telling the visiting church about the wasteland project. A few days later, I received a phone call from them to ask if we had ever dreamed of having an orchard to expand our jams and jellies program.

I said we had considered it briefly, but we had not made any concrete plans.

They carried that dream into reality, purchasing fifty fruit trees, planting them, staking them, and caring for them. We are now making jellies and jams from their fruit. When it is God's time, things simply fall into place.

THE ACCIDENT

It was a hot Saturday morning in July. I got up early and decided to make a pan of cinnamon rolls even though there were only two of us to eat them. I was in the mood and so I would give them away, or eat on them all weekend but I had a new recipe to try and this seemed like a good day to do it.

As we sat down to eat, my dogs began to bark. My gate is a long way from the house so I got up to see what they were barking at. Duke, a golden retriever, was running down the driveway toward a small child. I wasn't sure what the child wanted, but I knew that he would be frightened by such a big dog so I took off in pursuit.

I approached the child, and he asked me if I could help his Mama, she had gone off in the ditch. I gradually became aware of a car horn blaring. I looked in the direction that the noise was coming from and there in the creek bed, some seven feet down, was a car turned on its side. A leg was poked out the door of the car and I had flashbacks to the collapse of the bridge in Webber's Falls two months earlier when I had watched them extricate three cars and a horse trailer from the river bottom.

"Call 911" I yelled up to the house and I took off at a full run down the hill. The woman in the car was screaming and there was a second young boy coming up the hill toward me. "Are you alright?" I asked. "Yes," he responded.

"Go up to the house and take your brother with you," I said, "There is a nice lady there with some cinnamon rolls for you."

"I have to help my sister" he said. And he pointed to the car. There, hanging on the side of the car was a two-year old girl. She was screaming and very near falling from the side of the car into the creek bed.

I made it to the bridge beside the wrecked car trying to figure out if I should climb onto the car or go into the creek bed. The gas tank was torn open and gas was pouring out. I was terrified that the car would ignite and the children would witness their mother burn to death. I climbed down the embankment and grabbed the two year old and pulled. She slid easily off the edge of the car into my arms, screaming all the way. I handed her to her brother and told him to go now to the house for a cinnamon roll.

I then turned my attention to the mother. "Are you hurt?" I called.

"No", she returned, "but you have to save my baby".

With that, she pushed a six month old baby out of the car and slid her toward me. There was nothing to do but catch the baby and call her big brother back to get her. The mother was trying to get out of the car, but since it was on its side, she was fighting to hold the door open and find a place to brace herself to climb out. I ran to the garage, got a 2x4 to wedge in the door. I could hear sirens in the distance, but the leaking gas was such a threat that I continued to try to find ways to get the mother out. Finally, with all of the force we had left, I pried the door open enough for the mother to use both arms to lift herself out. She slid down to the ground and we ran until we were clear of the threat.

I helped the mother up to the house, told her to go in and have a cinnamon roll, and I went back to direct the emergency vehicles. As the fire trucks, ambulances, and County Sheriff's vehicles arrived, I began to realize how close this little family had come to serious injury or death. I thanked God for the protection that He gave throughout the entire ordeal. The EMT's went to check on the family and in a very short time they returned and loudly announced that there were fresh, homemade cinnamon rolls up at the house. When I finally returned to the house an hour later, hot, sticky and worn out, there was not one cinnamon roll left.

Even now, when I get in the mood to make cinnamon rolls on Saturday morning for no particular reason, I always stop and wonder who will show up to eat them.

"TAKE THREE"

I love communion! I love everything that it stands for, I love to take communion, and I love to serve communion. Communion is an opportunity for the people of God to gather at His table for a family meal. It is a time to re-tell the story of Christ and to remember how we became God's children. It is an opportunity to reflect upon our lives, to decide whether we like the things we are doing. It is the time to make changes if necessary, to make amends where needed, and to generally take stock of ourselves.

I believe that every person who is a child of God is welcome to share at the Lord's Table. Since there is no age requirement to being a child of God, there should not be an age requirement to communion. The last thing that we want is for our children to feel left out in their own church (and frankly, some of our children have a better grasp of grace than our adults) so all are invited if they want to come.

This practice can lead to some very entertaining situations from time to time. We take our bread and dip it in a common cup. There was the day that one of our little boys dropped his bread into the cup and proceeded to "fish" it out, all the way up to his wrist. Then there was the child who was being carried by her daddy. When he gave her the bread dipped in the juice her eyes lit up and she said in a loud voice, "Hey! That's good!"

It was Trish's first communion. She had come to the table with her family since she was a baby, but she never wanted the bread. One day, as she approached, I held the bread down and she took a piece and walked over to the cup as if she had being taking communion all of her life. I was so proud of her. She had finally made the step from observing to partaking. Others filed by, each taking a piece of bread while I gave words of encouragement. Suddenly, there she was again, taking a piece of bread, going over to the cup and dipping it in. I laughed to myself and continued. Several others passed by and there she was again. This time I glanced up to where her parents sat and her daddy was on the way to get her. We talked about it later and he assured me that she would take communion right from now on. "Is there a wrong way to take communion?" I asked?

Some may use this story as justification for *not* allowing the small children to come share, but we use it as a justification for why they should.

Trish's behavior is often shared as a family memory around our potluck tables. It holds valuable lessons for us in the telling. She was an onlooker for a long time, watching as others participated in the goodness and grace of our Lord Jesus Christ. How often we sit on the sidelines, wanting to be a part of the festivities, not really knowing how to become involved. We must become participants if we want to receive the blessings that God has to offer us.

I was enthused by Trish's drive for more, once she got a taste of the Lord's Supper. We need to revisit our early experience with Christ often, and remember how hungry we were to know everything about Him. We yearned to experience everything He had to offer and we couldn't wait to participate.

Finally, Trish learned how to take communion that day. Her daddy shared his faith and taught her the appropriate way to take communion. Her participation opened the door for a family discussion, for learning, and for sharing. Trish will remember, and share communion for a long, long time. What more could we ask?

AND MERI HAD A DONKEY!

Owning a donkey has always made life interesting and has offered lots of fodder for sermons and children's sermons.

My first donkey came as a complete surprise. I was hanging a fence around a pasture for the two horses I owned when a car pulled up and an older woman got out. She approached and told me she'd heard I had horses, and wondered whether I was interested in a donkey. It seems that her 92 year old father owned a house donkey...that's right!...the donkey opened the door to the house and came and went as she pleased.

Her father had fallen and broken his hip, and his daughter was concerned that the donkey would get in his way when he got home from the hospital. She worried he might fall again. She would give me everything that they had for the donkey; feed, a saddle, a water trough, if I would just give her a home.

I researched the compatibility of donkeys pastured with horses and discovered that it is a common practice. Donkeys are very protective of their turf and keep predators away. I decided that maybe this was a good thing, and June Bug came to live at the mission.

She attracted a lot of attention with work groups and guests who came to the mission. She even had an article published about her in the United Methodist Mission Magazine, "Response". In no time the entire community fell in love with her. The man who delivered donuts to the General Store across the street saved his day-old donuts for June Bug. She especially loved the chocolate filled kind. She would chew slowly and slurp the filling with a faraway look of pleasure in her eyes. When the old school building burned, it was June Bug who woke the community with her loud braying. I became Meri, the missionary with the donkey.

One church even adopted June Bug as their Vacation Bible School project and collected gifts for the mission using June Bug. They called and wanted to know if they could put her on speaker phone the night of their closing program. I explained to them that June Bug was a real donkey and she lived in a barn...no phones. They did call and a child from each class asked questions about June Bug. "How old is she?" "How long has she lived at the mission?" "Has she ever been baptized??????"

When June Bug died of cancer, it left a real void at the mission. My friends decided it just wasn't the same. Meri needed a donkey. They went to the sale barn and came home with an ornery young male donkey that I named

Eeyore. He was very short, but he loved to sneak up on the horses, bite them, and then run.

I kept the horses in a small paddock if the weather was bad and I'd had them pinned up for several days. The day had turned out pretty, so I decided I would let them out into the larger pasture. When the horses realized that they were free, they took off at a full run; around and around the pasture with Eeyore trailing behind. Every time they would lap him he would lay his ears back, bray, and run a little faster. Around and around they went, the horses making two laps to Eeyore's one. Finally, in frustration, he ran to where I was sitting on the fence watching and laid his head in my lap. His sides were heaving and he looked up at me with the most pitiful look.

"Eeyore," I said, "I know how bad you want to be a horse, but you are NOT a horse, you are a donkey. You will never be a horse, you will always be a donkey. God made you a donkey and God loves you because you are a donkey. There are some very special characteristics assigned to donkeys that horses don't have. It was a donkey that carried Mary to Bethlehem for the birth of Christ. It was a donkey that carried Jesus into Jerusalem. Donkeys may not be fast, but they are stout and sure footed. God made you special for purposes other than he made horses. God wants you to be who you are.

As I sat on the fence talking to Eeyore, I realized that there was a message there for me, as well. There are times when I wish I was someone else, when I wish that I looked different or did things differently, and I have to remind myself that God loves ME. God made me just the way I am and I don't have to be someone different.

Somehow Eeyore never grasped the concept of "missionary donkey". He never understood the legacy that was left to him. He did enjoy the donuts but it didn't take long before I realized that he was also enjoying the beer that some of the townspeople were giving him after I went to bed. I knew that it was time to take him to my ranch.

TRIAL BASIS

Communication is one of the most important ingredients of human understanding. We understand the situations we are in based on how the situation has been communicated to us. We understand people and their behavior based on the communication we establish with them.

I was visiting the County Jail one day to relate to the women incarcerated there and to see if they had any needs. I walked past one cell and there was a woman there that I had not met yet. I introduced myself and asked her if there was any way I could help her. One of the women in the cell next to hers yelled, "Don't bother with her, Preacher, she's crazy."

I chose to ignore her and continued with the woman in front of me. "Is there anything I can do for you?" I repeated.

"No," she replied. "I'm just in here on a trial basis to see if I like it. I am going to tell that judge that I don't like it here and I'm going home."

Unsure of what I just heard, I asked again. "I don't understand," I said. "I am a Pastor and if there is anything I can do for you, I will try."

"I told you, the judge told me he would put me in here for a few days and if I didn't like it I could go home. I'm going to tell him I don't like it and I'll get to go home tomorrow. I'm just here on a trial basis."

I was really confused. Common sense told me that judges didn't lock people up to see if they would like it. People weren't put into County on a trial basis.

"Well, if you decide you need something…" I repeated as I walked away.

On my way out of the jail, I stopped and asked the jailer what this woman meant. "She told me she was here on a 'trial basis'," I said.

The jailer laughed and said, "She is being held over for trial. We can't seem to convince her that it has nothing to do with whether she likes it or not."

BE CAREFUL WHAT YOU SAY

I had been working on the reservation for a couple of years when my father and a friend of his decided to come for a visit. His friend had an eight-year-old daughter who was very vocal in her resistance of going to the reservation. I finally asked her why she did not want to go and she told me she was afraid of Indians. In a half serious, half teasing voice I told her she didn't have a thing to worry about unless the Indians had on a war bonnet.

In all of the time that I had spent on the reservation, I had never seen anything but "civilian" clothing. We pulled up in front of the church and this little girl suddenly turned ashen, screamed and fell to the floor of the car. I looked in the direction of the church and there coming out of the church was the Pastor and a newspaper writer who had come to do a story on the mission. Walter was wearing a war bonnet. It was no easy task reassuring that little girl, let me tell you.

We are quick to judge based on appearances and information we have accumulated.

FLYING

I was flying into Dallas and was seated next to a mother and her young child. The child was looking out the window as we climbed, but it didn't take long until we were above the clouds. The flight lasted a little over an hour and the child stayed glued to the window. As we began to descend and came out of the clouds the little girl became excited and said, "It's ok Mommy, we're still in the air."

GETTING THE CONCEPT

On Easter Sunday I walked into the Church to put the finishing touches on the sanctuary. I always love the lilies and the draped cross. I was deep in thought and meditation when a six year old came running up to me with a new Children's Bible he'd received as an Easter gift. He wanted to show me all of the pictures. Finally, he came to a page and said, "Look Meri, this is where they nailed Jesus."

THERE ARE REASONS....

"NO! We don't crawl in under houses", I repeated for the fourth or fifth time. "If the floor is gone, we tear it out and work from the top. In this heat, there are apt to be snakes under there."

"Oh, hogwash!" one of the Volunteers responded. "I'm not afraid of snakes."

We were working on a one hundred year old log house that was about to tumble down. There was an addition on the side of the house where a bathroom had been added. It had pulled away from the wall and dropped a half a foot on the outside edge. The toilet sat at a 45° angle and the drains no longer drained. The roof had leaked at the separation and rotted both the roof and the floor below it. We needed to jack the addition up, re-attach it to the wall and fix the damage.

Before I could protest again, the man grabbed a jack, fell to the ground and squirmed in under the house. He was under there exactly five seconds when out he came, feet first. He jumped up and took off running down the dirt driveway. When we finally caught up to him he managed to tell us that there were two huge rattle snakes denned up under there.

"NO! We don't crawl in under houses....."

WHO'S IMPORTANT?

Eight year old Jeremy was sitting at my table for lunch. A cousin of his Dad's had been killed in a car wreck and the family needed me to take care of him and his older sister while all of the arrangements were being finalized and the funeral attended.

"Jeremy, would you like to ask the blessing?" I asked.

Jeremy began a journey through a rather lengthy discourse that included prayers for his dad and mom, prayers for the family, prayers for his pets that were "missing him." Finally he came to the part of his prayer that intrigued me. "And please be with Miss V. and make her better so that she can come back to church. I miss her. Amen." When he finished, I asked him which Miss V. he was praying for. There were two Miss V's in the church and both of them had been sick. He told me it was the one with the "broken leg".

The Miss V. with the broken leg was a quiet woman who could easily go unnoticed in the church. She walked with a cane and generally remained in the background. She had been sick with asthma for several Sundays now and had been unable to attend church. I suggested that we call Miss V. and tell her that Jeremy missed her in church. When she answered the phone they visited for a while and she told him that she missed him too, and hoped that she could come back to church soon.

That Tuesday Night when we all gathered for prayer at Bible Study, Jeremy asked for prayer once again for Miss V.

Wednesday dawned and Jeremy and his sister went home. That evening as I sat watching TV the phone rang. A frantic mother's voice at the other end of the line informed me that Trish, her three year old daughter, was sobbing, and had been crying for nearly an hour because she wanted to go to church. She'd told Trish there was nobody at church, but that only made her cry harder. I got on the phone and told Trish that there wasn't anyone at the church tonight, but we would all be there on Sunday to see her. Her exhausted little voice squeaked "ok" and she toddled off to bed. "She's fine," her mother told me, and then she thanked me for taking the time to talk to her.

I sat in my chair processing the conversation that I'd just had. A disturbing thought occurred to me; what if our children were not able to go to church if they wanted? What if there really was no one there--ever? What a joy and a blessing we have to worship at the church of our choice and in the style that suits us. I take that for granted too often.

Sunday came and Trish was there, grinning from ear to ear. "We get to go to church, today!" she told me. She had hardly walked by when Jeremy came running into the church shouting, "Miss V.'s here! Miss V.'s here! God answered my prayer…I made her better!" Now, despite the obvious flaw in his theology, my heart skipped a beat. This child had witnessed a prayer being answered, and he knew it.

Miss V. followed, and said to me, "I never knew that Jeremy was even aware of my presence at church…and to think that he was praying for me!"

My thoughts went directly back to Wednesday night. It can be so easy to make excuses for not attending church. There is so much to do, there are so many other places to go, we are tired, we need a break, our throats hurt. But what if we are the ones that the *children* are watching? What if there had never been anyone in church helping Jeremy to gain an understanding of prayer? What if we held church and nobody came?

We must never forget that every person in church is important…we are important…and God may be planning on using us to display His lesson for the day.

PARADISE OR HELL?

Sometimes things are just fun. It is an honor to be a part of a dedicated and committed group of people called Missionaries. In the United Methodist, there is a cadre of workers who call themselves Church and Community Workers. They are commissioned to go into remote areas of the United States and serve the community that has been left behind by the rest of society. When they have an opportunity to get together, they let their hair down, laugh and play, and release some of the stress that builds up in their jobs and their lives.

One such instance happened a few years ago when a group of Church and Community Workers gathered in Lancaster County, Pennsylvania, for a visit and a planning meeting. The Church and Community Worker assigned there had arranged for us to have an Amish meal in a town called Intercourse.

We loaded into a van and drove several miles to get to Intercourse. One of the guests in the van was a Pastor from Liberia. I have always been intrigued by other countries, so I struck up a conversation with him. We were discussing how appointments were made. He was serving a church in Michigan, so I asked him, "Does Michigan have a panhandle?" He expressed confusion, so I explained to him that the joke in Oklahoma is if a pastor crosses a District Superintendent or Bishop, their next appointment would be in the Oklahoma panhandle. Pastors who were appointed to the panhandle were teased about what behavior might have "earned" them this assignment.

He understood. He told me that in Michigan, if a Pastor was very good, there was a place called "Paradise" and the Pastor could look forward to serving in "Paradise" but if they were bad there was a place called "Hell, Michigan".....We all laughed and began surmising what kind of Pastoral faux pas would earn you the right to go to "Hell, Michigan."

As we entered the town of Intercourse, our attention turned to the town and the meal we could look forward to sharing together. The Liberian Pastor was obsessed with the name of the town. "Who would name a town Intercourse?" He asked, "Why would anyone name a town Intercourse? Imagine telling someone you are from Intercourse?"

He loved hearing himself say that, and of course with each question we all laughed a little harder. Finally he said, "Our Cabinet is meeting this week, I think I will write my Bishop and tell him, "While in the middle of Intercourse, I thought of you".

Gales of laughter filled the van. Without thinking, I turned and said, "And do you know what the Bishop will say to you? Daniel, go to Hell."

CHAPTER SIX

*"Bring the whole tithe
into the storehouse…"*
MALACHI 3:10

THE PUPPY

There is a young boy who has grown very dear to me. We do lots of things together and we spend a great deal of time talking and sharing together. He is delightful and I love to be with him.

I met him when he was moved into a foster care home at the age of eighteen months. He had a broken nose and cigarette burns on his legs. He was not potty training as quickly as his Grandfather thought he should, so he had been punished. He was removed from the home because of the neglect and abuse he suffered at the hands of his own family.

When he turned five, his foster family decided that he should have a puppy and they acquired a small female dog. I have a veterinarian friend and since the family did not want puppies, I was asked to take her to Muskogee, 60 miles away, to have her spayed. Of course, the child asked to go with me, and the plan was made. Because it was so far, we planned the entire day. We would take the dog to Lisa's, go to McDonald's to eat lunch, and play on the playground.

The day arrived and it was glorious! I gathered the dog carrier and my car keys, and loaded into the truck. It took a few minutes for us to catch the dog, but then we were on our way.

When we arrived, Lisa took the child under her wing and showed him all around her clinic. She had a red tail hawk that had been hit by a car and she had stitched its wing. She showed him her hedgehog, her cats, and her dogs. She explained the procedure as well as she could to a five year old and of course he wanted to know if "it will hurt?" The doctor put his puppy in a cage in the back room and I took the child by the hand. We turned to leave.

Suddenly, a howl came from the back room…a pitiful howl. Another, and then another. The puppy was crying and digging at the cage in an effort to get out. The child broke my hold on his hand and raced to the back of the clinic. You can imagine what a five year old child, loose in a veterinarian's office, could accomplish, so I ran after him.

There he was on his knees in front of that cage with the ear of his puppy in his little hand. This child, who had known only neglect and abuse, only anger and violence for the first eighteen months of his life was stroking the ear of that little puppy and saying, "Don't worry, Susie. I'm here for you 'cause I love you. Don't worry, Susie, I'm here for you 'cause I love you."

Later, as I pondered that moment over and over in my mind, it occurred to me that when Christians can lovingly take the hand of marginalized people; when Christians can take the hand of drug addicts and alcoholics, of poor and disabled, of the imprisoned and the lonely; when we can take the hand of all those in our society that need to experience the love and compassion of God, when we can take their hand and in all honesty and sincerity say to them, "Don't worry, I'm here for you, 'cause I love you. Don't worry, I'm here for you, 'cause I love you," then Christians will enter the true ministry and mission of Christ.   Amen

NELLIE JEAN

Nellie Jean was bedridden when I met her. She was in the final stages of cancer and everyday was a painful ordeal for her. She lived with her mother in a two room house with no running water and no electricity. The days were extremely hot and I know that Nellie Jean was very uncomfortable.

I had been sending in my entries to the Publisher's Clearing House Sweepstakes and I spent many hours, while I was driving to speaking engagements, planning how I would spend seven million dollars. I had it all planned out in my head, I would put some away for retirement or a rainy day. I would help each member of my family in a very specific way and I would give most of it to charities of my choice. I really enjoyed dreaming about the possibilities.

One of my staff was traveling with me one day, and so in the interest of conversation, I asked her what she would do with seven million dollars if she won the sweepstakes. She didn't answer right away so I jumped in and began to tell her all of the ways that I would be helpful if I won.

When I was finished, she quietly said, "I guess if I won seven million dollars I would use it in little ways to help people."

"Like what?" I inquired.

"Like Nellie Jean. I would have an electric line put into her house and I would buy her a TV so that she would have something to do during the long days."

I was really taken back. I realized that I had five TV's! I asked myself which one I was going to give to Nellie Jean. I started with the console in the living room, but that one was really too big. The one in the bedroom? Well, I watched that one the most. The one in the sewing room made it possible for me to watch there without hauling a unit in every time I wanted to sew. I had an old black and white, but I didn't feel right about giving her one that was not dependable. I had a really small one that I carried in the car, but of course, that one was not appropriate. Out of five TV's, I could not come up with a single TV that I could give to Nellie Jean.

I tell this story because I don't believe that I am the only one who would have struggled with this question. Sometimes we hold on so tightly to our possessions that even God can't pry them out of our hands.

The sad thing about that is, if God can't pry our things out of our hands, then He can't put anything back in them either.

Nellie Jean got her electric line. And her TV. And I didn't have to win the Sweepstakes to do it.

AND A LITTLE CHILD SHALL LEAD THEM

This past spring I received a note from one of our United Methodist Women with a check for $81.00 in it. Now ordinarily $81.00 is not a large gift, but it is one that will always be appreciated. As I read the note, my eyes began to tear. The note went like this:

"This money was raised by a seven year old girl. She saved her allowance and other gifts. Her name is Jessica. Use her gift to help other children not so fortunate as she."

This was the second year that this child had saved ALL of her money and sent it to Cookson for other children. This child's generosity and sensitivity to the needs of others is overwhelming for a youngster her age. What a wonderful example to us all.

WE CAN'T PAY THE BILLS!

It was nearing the end of the fiscal year and we still owed the projects' portion of my salary to the General Board of Global Ministries. We were not going to have nearly enough cash to pay the insurance, the salaries and my field share. My Administrative Assistant was standing in my office delivering the bad news.

"What are we going to do?" she asked. "I know that you always tell me that God will take care of it, but heck, Meri, this is serious! We need at least $17,000 by the end of next week."

It was not the first time that we had been faced with a serious shortfall of cash, but it was certainly the worst. I told her to give me the weekend to think about it and we would discuss it on Monday.

The weekend was difficult for me. I prayed, I argued, I processed. I figured several options but nothing met with my approval. "God," I prayed, "what are we going to do? I can't lay people off this close to Christmas. I can't borrow the money, that would just make it worse. I don't know where to turn. I don't know what to do."

I finally decided that the only option was to throw ourselves at the mercy of the General Board and hope that they would forgive the debt, or at least extend payment.

We had our usual staff meeting on Monday morning and I told them what a difficult position we were in and what we were going to try. I explained that I really didn't know what we would have to do if we couldn't work it out with the General Board. We prayed as a staff and quietly got up to begin our work.

The phone rang as we were gathering up our belongings. I was the first one to return to my office so I picked it up.

"Cookson Hills Center, may I help you?" I asked.

"I am looking for a Rev. Whitaker," said the voice at the other end of the line.

"I'm Rev. Whitaker." I continued.

"I'm a lawyer from Oklahoma City," he said. "I have some good news for you. One of my clients died, well that's not good, but they left some money to your mission."

My heart skipped a beat. "Really?" I asked. I couldn't believe my ears.

"Now don't get excited. It's not that much, just fifty dollars."

My heart sank. "That's alright," I told him, "fifty dollars is fifty dollars. We operate on small gifts. We don't get many big gifts."

"I'm kidding!" he responded with pleasure. "It is really $35,000!!!"

I was jubilant as I gathered the staff back in the main room. We thanked God for answering our prayer.

When it is God's time, things just fall into place.

MARY LEE DAVIS

I once knew a woman named Mary Lee Davis. Mary Lee was elderly, she had very bad hygiene and her clothes were old and dirty. She loved to talk, and talk, and talk. She would walk into the church, pick out someone who looked available, walk up to them and almost hold them hostage as she talked about anything that crossed her mind. If you stood at a distance you could see people move out of her path and almost hide to avoid her.

The church was very good to her at holidays. A basket was always prepared and delivered to her. She lived a very humble lifestyle and everyone believed that she was indigent.

Mary Lee died in 1975 and her belongings were packed up to go into a dumpster or to a local charity. No one ever expected to find a will, but there was one. Mary Lee Davis left this often insensitive church $85,000.

I WISH I HAD A MILLION BUCKS

It was a hot dusty afternoon. I was sitting on a picnic table visiting with the senior citizens as they left the nutrition program one afternoon. The breeze was stifling and gave no relief to the heat and the humidity. Some of the folks would take a few minutes to visit and others would nod and hurry on with places to go and errands to run.

Harley sat down on the table next to me and we shared the usual pleasantries. "Hi, how are you?" "How's your day going?" It was a rather benign conversation and I wasn't expecting any deep revelations.

Harley stared off into space and announced that he wished he had a million bucks. "Boy, if I had a million bucks I could sure live a different life...I could take better care of my grandkids, I could put running water in my house, I could fix my roof...if I had a million bucks........"

His voice drifted off and he stared off again and then he said, "Ahh, I don't know what I'm talking about, I don't need no million bucks. I ain't never seen anybody who had that kind of money that was happy either."

MAXINE

It happened just today. The weather was beautiful, sunny, and 82°. The wind was blowing, but there is a promise in the air that spring has arrived. The redbuds are in full bloom and the flock, daffodils and tulips are just beautiful.

We had entertained a United Methodist Women's Group for our Senior Citizen's lunch and they had been given a tour. I sat with them during the meal to attempt to address the many questions they had. I was running a little late delivering my "take out" meal and it was a long drive to the home of the woman that needed this lunch.

As I rounded the corner and headed for my car one of our regular attendees called to me and asked if I could give her a few minutes of time. I glanced at my watch and stepped over to her.

I had known Maxine for many years. She used to come to the Center, as a young woman, when her children were babies. She had used the services of the Center when she got sick and had a heart attack. We built a ramp into her trailer when she had to have a leg amputated as the result of her diabetes. She has always been one of our craft workers and so we have had a long relationship.

She motioned to me to come close and she said, "I need to tell you something."

My first instinct was a feeling of foreboding. What was wrong? What was she upset about? But I let her continue, and she said, "When I die, I want you to know that you need to follow up with Cherokee Nation. I have taken out a life insurance policy for $25,000 and Cookson Hills is the beneficiary."

I looked at this little woman who had suffered poverty and physical illness her whole life. This was a woman who had never had $500 at one time just to spend, and my eyes filled with tears. "Oh, Maxine," I said, "you don't need to do that, what about your daughter?"

"I took one out for her, too," she replied, "I just wanted to do this 'cause ya'll have done so much for me all these years. I can't do nothing in this life but you will get something from me when I die."

I did not know what to say, I mumbled something about that being a long way off, but both of us knew it wasn't. I realized that giving is important to everyone. There are those whose life doesn't allow for much giving. In fact, it seems that taking is all that they do, and yet deep within the heart of every person is the desire to feel the joy of giving.

Realizing this, it becomes my responsibility to find ways that the economically disadvantaged can be given opportunities to give, for in giving, we receive.

Thanks Maxine!!

GOD STILL SPEAKS

1 Samuel 3:9

"Speak, Lord, for your servant hears."

I sat under the open air arbor as the hot breeze stirred the campgrounds. I watched a tarp that was serving as a sun shade rise and fall with the wind as swirls of dust filled the space underneath it. Sitting with me were two hundred American Indian Pastors and Delegates from Tribes all over Oklahoma. The singing of traditional hymns in languages like Kiowa, Cherokee, Creek and Choctaw filled my soul and drew me to a place long ago when these hymns were the only ones sung by Tribal Christians, whose lives were much harder than most of us can imagine.

It was time for the Oklahoma Indian Missionary Conference in Antlers, Oklahoma. The Conference takes place the second week of June and rotates through three different locations; Anadarko, Preston and Antlers. Annual Conference is a time for fellowship, a time for beans, fried potatoes, and hog fries, made in huge cast iron skillets over an open fire. A time for the business of the church and a time for worship.

I was struggling with a report given earlier in the day. The United Methodist Women were working toward taking a trip to Alaska to teach Vacation Bible School. In the midst of the report, they had the women who were going stand and be recognized. I had locked in on an elderly woman whose face portrayed the ultimate characteristics of age; gentleness, and understanding. There was something in that face that I simply couldn't get out of my mind.

As I sat in the heat of the day, a voice inside of me kept saying, "Give an anonymous gift to her expenses." I was willing to give, but the figure of $200 kept coming to mind. "I'll give $50," I thought.

"No! $200!"

"No, that's too much, $75," I reasoned.

"No! $200!"

"Okay! $100."

"$200!"

I don't know why that was such a struggle. $200 dollars at that time was a lot of money and I seldom ever gave that much to anything, but this persistent little voice would not give up. I went to town, cashed a check, and put

$200 dollars in a plain envelope. I wrote her name on it and took it to her District Superintendent with instructions to put it toward her expenses. It was done, but the debate in my head was not over. It was a large amount of cash. I replayed arguments over and over, for and against the practicality of such a donation.

The next night in the middle of the worship service, an elderly champion of the faith stood and began to speak. "I have wanted to go to Alaska more than anything. I have saved $5.00 every month for a year to be able to go, but my husband and I have figured out that even if I save $5.00 a month until it is time to go, I would still not have enough. I would still be $200 short. We had decided that I would not be able to go. But today, one of you, I don't know who, gave my D.S. exactly $200. Now I can go to Alaska. Whoever you were, thank you."

Everyone stood clapping and cheering. No one noticed this humble missionary sitting on a back pew with tears running down her face, thanking God for the message and persistence of that still, small voice.

THE GIFT OF BICYCLES

I am often asked to be a guest preacher in churches all across this country to promote the work that we are doing at the Cookson Hills Center. The very best way to do that is to tell stories of the activities and people at the Center. One such Sunday I was telling about a family that was dirt poor. They had no running water, they lived in a very humble home, food was scarce and there were very few, if any, toys. At the conclusion of the service a man approached me and handed me a check to go and buy each of the children a new bike. This is always awkward for me because I don't want anyone to think that I play favorites with our children but I also hesitate to refuse any gift offered to avoid hurting the feelings of the giver.

I accepted his gift and went into town the next day to buy the bikes. I found three that were similar and loaded them into the truck. After lunch I decided to take the bikes out to the family. There was a group visiting us from the east and they had a pastor leading them. I asked her if she would like to ride along with me to deliver the bikes. She enthusiastically said yes.

As we drove along we visited some and then she started to get wound up. She said she just couldn't wait to get to the house. She just couldn't wait to see the faces of the children when they saw the bikes. She wondered if they knew how to ride bikes. She couldn't wait to see how excited they were going to be! Finally, I told her that the children would not even be there. I deliberately chose this time to go because they would be in school.

She looked confused and disappointed. I explained to her that the bikes were not our gifts to give and that we did not even know if the parents wanted the children to have the bikes. The bikes would be given to the parents to decide what to do. They might want to wait and give them as Christmas gifts, they might not want the children to even have a bike. If the children were there when we arrived we would have eliminated the parents right to choose.

I firmly believe that as "caregivers" it is our job to empower others to determine their futures. We are "caregivers," not saviors. When we rush in to fix every problem, when we see ourselves as saviors, the hidden implication is that others need to be saved and that erodes self esteem. I believe that people need a hand up, we don't need to carry them. One more important consideration was that I didn't want these children to see me as some sort of "fairy godmother" who could give them things that their parents were unable to give. The more we "save," the more we harm. One of my favorite quotes is from John Wesley; "Do no harm."

We pulled up in front of the house and were greeted by the parents. I told them that I had three bikes in the back of my truck and they could have them if they wanted. They were elated and enthusiastically accepted them. I don't know if the pastor ever really understood what I was saying to her or whether her disappointment dominated her feelings. To this date, I do not know what the parents did with the bikes, I do not know if they saved them for Christmas, or if they gave them to the children immediately.

All I know is the image I conjured up in my own head of the children's reaction and that will carry me for a long time.

CHAPTER SEVEN

*"…You have plenty of good things laid up
for many years. Take life easy; eat,
drink, and be merry."*
LUKE 12:19

PERSONAL MESSAGES SHOULD BE
KEPT TO ONESELF

The women of the Church are famous for giving "in-kind" gifts. They love to gather baby items, knit mittens, or quilt blankets for those less fortunate than themselves. I believe that they immerse themselves in empathy of the recipient as these gifts of love are distributed. They can see children try on their new mittens, and squeal with delight as they are given a hat to match. They can feel the appreciation as blankets are given to the elderly. To the women of the church, giving gifts to missions comes as naturally as breathing.

One year the United Methodist Women of the Oklahoma Conference decided to collect underwear and socks for the children of Cookson Hills. They arrived by parcel post, by mail and by individual delivery. I picked up a van load at the Women's Annual Meeting, and brought back the collections from smaller churches I was visiting. It was wonderful to receive all of these gifts, and to plan ways to distribute them.

The United Methodists of each Annual Conference gather once a year to hear reports on extension ministries, vote budgets, fellowship, and take care of any other church business. Each church selects a delegate and an alternate to represent them We were meeting in Okmulgee and the First United Methodist Church of Okmulgee had called to say that they would leave their collection of underwear and socks at the front desk of the hotel. Our delegates from Canterbury (both men) had gone on ahead. I was traveling with the staff from Cookson.

We arrived at the hotel and my administrative assistant stepped up to the desk to check in. I was greeted by friends that I had not seen all year and we were catching up on the year's activities when Donna interrupted to tell me that I had a message at the desk.

"Here," I said, "let me read it."

"Oh, no," she responded, "I'll read it." With that she shook out the paper very ceremoniously and read at the top of her voice:

"Rev. Whitaker, your underwear is in the men's room."

DO I HAVE TO EAT THAT?

Food was always an issue in our house when I was growing up. My dad grew up as a poor sharecropper's son in Mississippi, then was a sergeant in the Air Force providing for seven children. We ate simple, home cooked meals planned on a budget. Mom made our bread, our biscuits, our cornbread. We had soups, stews and casseroles. I was never asked if I liked what was served, it was dinner. We were expected to eat it.

I forced down many meals that I found no pleasure in eating. I was unaware of how God was preparing me to go on the mission field. When you enter a world that is different from your own, you must expect that the food will also be different than yours. Some will be very tasty and some will not.

While I was in Anadarko, I had the occasion to try kidney gravy. I do not like kidney gravy, but every time we had a church gathering one of the members of the congregation would bring kidney gravy and make mention of its presence at the table. I always ate the gravy, in an attempt to be polite, as everyone watched me. I am not sure whether they really thought I liked the gravy or whether they knew I didn't and were having a little fun with me, but I ate it and it had no adverse effects on me.

****

Birthdays are always a time of celebration. I had not been on the mission field for more than a few months when I was invited to my first birthday party. It was for one of the children in my program and I was delighted to be included. One of the veteran missionaries confided in me that the older men of the Kiowa Tribe enjoyed eating kidney, liver and heart........raw. They only ate it on special occasions, but it would be very offensive if I refused to try it if they offered some to me. This caused me some concern and frankly, it took some of the excitement away from the party. I wasn't sure I could eat raw meat, no matter who offered it. I worried, I prayed, I talked to myself, what should I do???

Finally, the day of the party came. We gathered for a cookout in the park. The children were playing, the women were cooking and the men were visiting at a picnic table some distance away. I moved around striking up a conversation with people, all the while keeping my distance from the group of older gentlemen.

Then, the moment came that I had been dreading. One of the men spotted me and summoned me over to the table. With a resigned sigh, I began to make my way over to the table where I knew they were eating raw kidney. I

140

was almost there when one of the grandmothers stepped out, caught me by the arm and asked me to come help her get the food ready. I let my breath out as I realized that she had deliberately rescued me from what could have been a very ugly scene...my prayers had been answered.

****

Easter lived on a dirt road way out in the country. It would have been impossible to find her without specific directions. The home was an old log cabin built by her father over a hundred years ago. She was ninety three years old, spoke no English and had never lived anywhere else. The house needed repairs, so I had taken a work team out there. We had been working for a week and were finishing up when Easter appeared with a cake she had baked.

Easter had no running water, so her kitchen was not scrubbed clean. She had no counter space, she worked off an old homemade wooden table. She cooked on an old woodstove. It was July in Oklahoma so heating up the stove to bake a cake made the entire house unbearable. Easter lived on less than $1,000 a year, so a cake was a treat that she was very proud of. She began to cut the cake and asked our translator to invite the group to come and have a piece. It was an orange cake with orange icing.

One by one the group made excuses for not having a piece of cake: they weren't hungry, it was too hot, they were on a diet, they didn't eat orange. My interpreter and I took a piece of cake and sat down under a tree to eat it. I have never tasted a cake as good in my life! It melted in your mouth. I went back for seconds and then I found myself going back for thirds. It was delicious. Secretly, I was glad the group didn't want any, it left more for me.

****

Oklahoma winters can be cold! The wind was blowing and the snow was falling at an unprecedented rate. Charlie and I put the chains on the truck and loaded up groceries and blankets to take to the elderly. I wanted to be sure that they had wood inside to heat their homes with and that they had plenty of food in case we didn't get back out for a while. We arrived at one of our homes and were invited to come in. Nattie, age eighty seven, was sitting in front of her wood stove in a rocking chair with a blanket wrapped around her. She was chewing tobacco and spitting at the stove. The stove made a hissing sound when she hit it. She never missed.

I had been around lots of people who chewed tobacco, and I had observed many different containers used for "spit cups". Pop cans, paper cups, bottles, and tin cans were all used for spitting into. Nattie asked us if we wanted a cup of coffee. It was cold outside, so of course we wanted a cup of coffee. Besides, it would be impolite to refuse. She had to go outside to the well to bring in water and I knew that her coffee supply was limited so offering a cup was a pretty big sacrifice.

My stomach sank when she brought out the coffee. There were things floating in it. I just knew that she had mistakenly brought me her "spit cup." What could I do? I didn't want to embarrass her by pointing this out. I didn't want to waste her valuable coffee and I certainly didn't want to offend her. My insides roiled as I tried to sip on the coffee. I managed to force down about half a cup, all the while believing I was drinking from her "spit cup".

I was sick to my stomach as we drove home. Finally, Charlie asked me if I was alright. When I told him what had happened, he burst into gales of laughter. I really thought we were going to drive off the road into a ditch! *I* certainly didn't think it very funny, until Charlie explained that the "old timers" didn't use strainers or coffee baskets to make coffee, they simply threw a handful of coffee into a pot and brought it to a boil. That wasn't tobacco after all, it was coffee grounds.

I can't help thinking about the Scripture in Romans 14:14 where Paul says,

> *"do not by your eating destroy your brother for whom Christ died…for the Kingdom of God is not about eating or drinking, but righteousness and peace and joy in the Holy Spirit."*

Life often puts us into situations that are not palatable or are hard to swallow. Our job is to do the best we can without offending anybody. It is not always "about us", sometimes we are expected to reach deep inside ourselves and find a strength we didn't know we had to meet these situations head on. That strength comes from the Holy Spirit. When we put the needs of others first, when we struggle with the things in life that are not pleasurable, we come to know firsthand what "righteousness, peace and joy in the Holy Spirit" means.

WHAT KIND OF CEREAL DO YOU LIKE?

A mother shared this story with me one day.

Her little boy got up and was ready for breakfast. In an effort to begin his day on a positive note, she asked him what kind of cereal he would like.

Without batting an eye he replied, "Fruit of the loops."

WHALE MEAT IN OKLAHOMA?

Throughout the summer there were several groups that came to visit and work either teaching Vacation Bible School or painting, building and repairing churches. These are a few stories that came from these groups.

One week, late in the summer, we had a visiting group from Upstate New York come to teach Vacation Bible School. I had the responsibility of showing them around and so one afternoon we decided that we would take a trip to the mountains just outside of Lawton. There is a little town there named Mears that is famous for being the smallest town in the U.S. It is a single building with a Post Office and a restaurant. There is one parking meter out front but the meals at the restaurant are super!

The main menu is beef-Texas Longhorn, but they serve some buffalo as well. We stopped for dinner and we were reading the wall (the menu is painted on the wall) when one of the girls said to me, "I didn't know they had whale meat here." "Whale meat!" I exclaimed, "Where do you see whale meat?" She insisted that the whale meat was up on the wall and she tried to get me to spot it. I just didn't see it and I couldn't believe that Mears, OK. served whale meat. Finally, in frustration, I said, "Go up and point to it, I don't see it."

The girl went to the wall and said, "Whale meat, right here, fried Orca." I looked at the item she was pointing to and I started to laugh as I told her, "That's fried okra."

CAN YANKEES REALLY ADAPT TO OKLAHOMA?

I was at the closing VBS program of one of the Indian Churches and we were sharing in a potluck dinner. Someone had brought yellow watermelon, which looks like watermelon, tastes like watermelon and even cuts like watermelon, but instead of being red in the middle it is yellow. One of the participants in the group looked at the yellow melon and asked me what it was. I told him it was "squash melon". He said he had never had "squash melon" but it sounded interesting so he would try it. A few minutes later he told me that the "squash melon" was very good. It even tasted a lot like squash!

KITTEN FOR DINNER?

One evening in Western Oklahoma I had scheduled a youth activity, so I was "running the route" picking up teenagers for the event. I pulled into one house and the youngest child was sent out to tell me they weren't ready yet, but they would be right out. I started a conversation with the child and asked her what she was doing. She told me she was getting ready to eat, so I asked the obvious next question. "What are you going to have?"

"Kitten" she replied.

"KITTEN!???" I was distressed. "You're having kitten?" I just couldn't imagine anyone being forced to eat kitten. I asked her three times to be sure I heard her right and each time she emphatically told me they were having kitten. I was sick. Of all things, to eat a kitten! Why would they eat a kitten and not wait for it to grow up and fatten up to a full sized cat?!? I stewed over this information for a week until I couldn't stand it any longer. I asked the missionary couple who had served Anadarko for years how they could allow families to eat kitten.

I knew by the puzzled look on her face that I had stepped into a subject that she was uncertain how to handle. She quizzed me several times on what I had heard this child say...YES!!! She was eating kitten, I insisted. We checked the date of the youth event and she went in to call the family because she was certain that none of our families ate kitten. She returned from her phone call laughing until the tears were rolling down her face...it seems that they were having kidney not kitten. I had spent a very unhappy week for nothing.

WHAT'S SHE WORTH?

A young mother came into my office with her four year old son and her brand new baby daughter. I made a fuss over the baby, held her, and then put her back into the carrier she had come in. Then I turned my attention to the boy.

"Is this your baby?" I asked.

He nodded his head, so I asked, "Can I have her?"

This time the child shook his head no.

"I'll give you a dollar," I continued.

Again he shook his head no.

"I'll give you five dollars."

He still shook his head no.

"I'll give you a horse," I bargained unrelentingly.

This time he ran over to the carrier and began dragging it over to me. His mother and I laughingly told him that a horse for his sister was not a fair exchange! He left with the same sister he'd come with.

THE DOVE

Sunday School is such a delightful time for children to learn and to respond to the stories that were the foundation of our faith.

The story for the week was Noah and the Ark. This is a story that is repeated often to children and grabs their imagination because of all the animals that Noah lived with on the ark.

Jean, the Sunday School teacher, was quizzing the children on what they had learned that day. "How long was Noah on the ark?" she asked. "What animal did Noah send out to see if the water was gone?" she continued.

To each question, John gave the proper response. He had listened well.

"Forty days," he answered. Then, "A dove."

"And what did the dove bring back so that Noah would know that the water was all gone?" She asked.

"A note!" John yelled.

NOAH AND THE ARK

It was the time in the service for the children's sermon. We were still in the old sanctuary, a cold and drafty place. The front door had a hole in the bottom. I had decided to tell the story of Noah and the Ark to the children that day. I began by explaining to them how God told Noah to build an ark. Noah had never seen a boat. He didn't know what he was doing, but he did what God asked.

Then God told him to go and gather up two of every kind of animal and put them on the boat. Just as I said "two of every animal", two mice scurried across the front of the altar area, under my legs and out the hole in the door. The children screamed, I jumped up and the adults all tried to get a better look. None of us will ever forget the "real" illustration of the animals coming two by two.

WHEN SCORPIONS FLY

The mission trip to Arizona was coming to a close and our youth had learned many things. We were to spend the night in Anadarko at the American Baptist Camp Grounds. This is a facility used for "camp meeting" each summer. The surrounding churches gather for a week of preaching, eating and fellowship. Everyone camps and it is a wonderful time.

I had explained to the youth that there were snakes, scorpions, and tarantulas that inhabited Oklahoma and so they must be careful and be aware. We pulled into the campgrounds after dark and unloaded the cars. Girls seldom go to the restroom alone and so they asked if they could all go to the restroom together. After cautioning them that there were people who had already gone to bed and were asleep, I said yes and they headed off for the primitive bathroom. They hadn't been gone five minutes when I heard loud piercing screams coming from the bathroom.

"Scorpion! Scorpion!" they screamed as they ran out of the bathroom. "There's a scorpion flying around down there!"

I had seen a lot of things in my time, but honestly, I had never seen a scorpion fly. I didn't even know they had wings. This I had to see for myself. I went down to the bathroom after scolding the girls for making so much noise. Of course, the girls were hanging on to me as we went. Upon our arrival, they pointed out the "flying scorpion" and I laughingly told them that this bug was a locust. Big? Yes. Ugly? Yes, but not a flying scorpion.

Later, that night, we settled into our bedrolls but the girls just wouldn't relax. They just knew that a scorpion, or a copperhead, or some other "wild" animal was going to get into the cabin and attack them while they slept. Finally, in the interest of a little rest, I told them that scorpions glowed in the dark. They had nothing to fear, they could see a scorpion from across the room. Things got very quiet, the light was turned off, and it appeared that we could finally get some much-needed sleep.

It was then that I reached into my sleeping bag and quietly took out my "glow in the dark" key chain and pushed it toward the girls. "Girls," I said. Immediately the cabin erupted into screams of terror. The male counselor who had accompanied us, jumped out of bed to turn on the light. He was a rather stout man and had gone to bed in his shorts. He flipped on the light, realized that he was not dressed and flipped off the light, again. The girls screamed and begged, but there was no way he was going to turn that light back on.

Flying scorpions, glow-in-the-dark scorpions! I still get tickled when I think of the imagination of these teenage girls.

DON'T BE ALARMED

I love living in the country. I have been a city dweller, I have lived in the suburbs, but I really believe that the country is my natural habitat. Living in the country does set one back though, when it comes to keeping pace with technology and all of the new "gadgets" that are continually coming out to make life simpler.

I still haven't learned how to record on my VCR and now there is some new thing called a DVR. I don't have a cell phone, but that is alright because no one who comes to the ranch to visit can get a "signal?" anyway.

Bearing that in mind, I will never forget the time a friend of mine came to visit driving a new SUV. She had parked it in the pasture next to the driveway and walked up to the house. I fixed iced tea and we prepared to sit on the front porch. I told her that she might want to bring the car a little closer to the house because the donkey had a history of finding articles on cars that he liked to chew on. He loved to suck on the hood ornament on my brother-in-law's El Camino. He enjoyed chewing windshield wipers. He found pleasure in scratching his back on anything that protruded from the car...mirrors, antennas, license plates.

"Oh, that's ok," she explained. "This car has an alarm on it. If he touches any part of the car, the alarm will sound."

I sat back to enjoy the day and visit with my friend, reassured that the donkey could do no harm to her new vehicle.

It wasn't long before I spotted him approaching the SUV with his ears up. Sometimes I wish that I could read the minds of my animals, but this time it wasn't necessary. He was perfectly transparent. He had spotted something brand new in his pasture and that made it "fair game" to investigate and help himself to anything that he found pleasurable.

He strolled up to the automobile without hesitation and looked it over from bumper to bumper. We watched with interest as he assessed the possibilities of this new, shiny guest. Then he reached up and stuck his nose on the door. A high pitch alarm began to sound, Whew...whew...whew...whew.

Eeyore spun around and ran down the pasture as fast as his short little legs would carry him. He ran about a hundred yards and whirled around to face his attacker. The alarm had a control on the key ring, so it was a simple matter to press a button to turn it off. I couldn't control my laughter and looked down the field to see what had become of my little donkey.

Here he came…ears laid back…head to the ground…sneaking up on this car that had given him such a scare. We watched as he circled the car once again and obviously found it to be no threat so he reached up once again and touched the door. The alarm sounded and he turned and fled down the pasture once again.

This time he did not go quite as far away when he spun around, laid his ears back and began to sneak up on the intruder once more. We spent an hour watching this scene played over and over, and we laughed until tears poured down our faces as time after time this little donkey tried to win the battle over this car.

As hard as it is to believe, there is a lesson in this comical story. I learned, by watching Eeyore, that it is essential to follow through on things that are important to us. We allow fear to stall us and intimidation to bring our interest in life to a grinding stop. Eeyore was afraid and ran away, but he always came back.

There are many times in my life that I know that God is calling on me to act a certain way, to say a certain thing, or even to go somewhere. We are so afraid that God will ask us to do something that is too hard, or will make us miserable, that we don't even investigate the possibilities. We can learn from this little donkey; to confront our fears, to address them, and to be persistent in conquering the things in this life that intimidate us.

CHAPTER EIGHT

*"Today in the town of David,
a Savior has been born to you;
He is Christ the Lord."*

LUKE 2:11

MISS FLOSS

There is a woman in our area named Miss Floss, who is one of my favorites to visit. Miss Floss lives in a little shotgun house with a tin roof. It is old and it is drafty. She still cooks on a wood stove and it keeps her house nice and warm year round. Miss Floss is a tiny woman, about 4'8" in stature and weighs in at 97 pounds. She has arthritis so bad her fingers form a 90° angle to her hand.

Miss Floss has no teeth and she loves to chew tobacco. Being toothless makes that difficult for most people, but Miss Floss chews her tobacco into a piece of bubble gum. When she gets tired of chewing she takes the gum out and rolls it between her fingers and her thumb. Miss Floss is fluent in both English and Cherokee, but she forgets who she is talking to and moves from one language to another within her conversation. She is often hard to understand.

We worked on her home one summer, putting a new roof on it. I made a visit to her home the following spring and as we were sharing a cup of coffee, I kept hearing birds chirping. "Miss Floss?" I asked in concern. "Do you have a hole somewhere, I hear birds."

She laughed and replied, "No, them be those baby chicks you gave me. I kept stepping on 'um and a killing 'um, so I took the ones that was left and put them in the bed where they are warm and they can't run around." She turned down the covers of her bed and there were four baby chicks hidden under three quilts.

On Christmas we always go caroling at Miss Floss's house. This particular year we went to her house with a group of teenagers. Miss Floss was always cold, so in the winter she lived in her kitchen/bedroom with the wood stove fired up as high as it would go. She came out into the living room to hear the kids sing, and when they were finished they asked her what she wanted for Christmas. She looked puzzled, then thoughtful, and finally said, "I want a piece of bubble gum and two oranges." This humble request had a strong impact on the teenagers.

As we were ready to leave, I told Miss Floss that I would help her back into the bedroom. As we let the kids out and started that way, Miss Floss started to holler. I asked her what was wrong and realized that her pants had fallen down around her ankles. We laughed together, and I bent down and pulled them back up for her. We took a few more steps and she started to holler again…they had dropped to the floor again. I bent down and pulled up her pants for the second time and this time we continued with me trying to hold on to her and hold up her pants at the same time.

We got tickled and started to laugh. She said, "What if people could see us now!?" As we finally made our way to the bedroom, got her settled into her chair and added some wood to her fire, I said, "Miss Floss, we gotta get you some pants with some elastic in them. You can't keep pulling these up."

Miss Floss looked at me and said, "Honey, I'm just thankful to have a pair of pants to pull up."

She could have been bitter about her poverty, but she wasn't. She could have been bitter about her age, but she wasn't. She rejoiced in her circumstances and as a result she gave God a *great* song to sing.

God is indeed in our midst, to save us, to quiet us, to sing over us. What song have we given Him this week?

MAUDE AND PEARL

Christmas caroling has become an activity that has been all but lost. We still see it in the movies, like Charles Dickens's *A Christmas Carol,* where a group of folks in long dresses and mufflers gather around the light pole to sing. But there are so few people who find the time to go caroling anymore that it is almost forgotten.

A group of girls wanted to carol for the elderly of Cookson, so I agreed to take them out to some homes. I always went out the day of the activity, to inform folks that we were coming so that they would not go to bed or be frightened.

Maude and Pearl were ninety-three and ninety-two years old, respectively. Maude still drove a little yellow Hornet whenever she felt she needed to go someplace. We were constantly having to pull her out of a ditch. One day she drove the car over a big rock in our parking lot and we had to jack the car up to push it off.

They were a very old fashioned and independent lot, and I felt that they were good candidates for our caroling group to go to. I drove out to their house and asked permission to bring the group there that evening. They were delighted, so I told them that we would be there around seven thirty or eight.

I was so proud of myself. We were right on schedule and arrived in Maude and Pearls' driveway at exactly seven-thirty. I told the girls to stay in the car while I went to the door, and I would signal them when Maude and Pearl were ready. I rang the bell. No answer. I knocked. No answer. I knocked a little louder. No answer. I could hear the TV on in the living room and the car was in the driveway, so I knew that they were there. I began to get concerned and decided that I would knock one more time and if I didn't get a response, I would leave and call the police.

This time I really pounded, just in case they couldn't hear me over the blaring TV. "Who is it?"

I was relieved to finally get a response. "It's me, Meri, Maude."

"Who?" she asked.

"Meri," I replied. "We've come to sing to you."

"Well, you damned near got your head blowed off," she retorted. With that she opened the door. She was holding a huge pistol, pointing it right at me.

"Maude!" I exclaimed. "I told you that we were coming tonight to sing some Christmas Carols for you and Pearl."

"Yeah, well, I forgot!" she ended.

Thinking back on it, perhaps I can understand why Christmas Caroling is becoming a thing of the past. It would be a shame if we quit doing it all together, but needless to say, that was the last time that we caroled for Maude and Pearl.

I'M NOT PREGNANT!

Early December was, of course, a very busy time at the church as it prepared for Christmas. I was rushing from Sunday School to the sanctuary when one of our three year olds stepped out in front of me, looked up and said, "You're gonna have a baby."

I was dumbfounded. "No, I'm not!" I responded emphatically. A single pastor certainly doesn't need to have that kind of rumor going around.

"Yes, you are. My teacher said so." The child returned.

"No, I'm not!" I said again.

Rather than continue an argument with a three year old who was convinced he was right, I took him by the hand and went back into his Sunday School classroom. I found his teacher and told her that this child insisted she'd said I was going to have a baby. She denied any such statement.

The child jumped in, very upset, and said, "Yes! You did, you said Mary was going to have a baby and name him Jesus."

"Wrong Mary!" We said together in obvious relief. "Mary lived a long time ago…she was a different Mary."

I KNEW SOMEBODY WOULD COME THROUGH

"Tonight will be the coldest night of the year," the weatherman announced. "It will get down to 2° F."

I was preparing to make my last deliveries for Christmas, then was headed home to a warm fire, a cup of coffee, and the holidays. Just as I was leaving, my phone rang. It was a young mother with two very small children. She was behind in her rent and her landlord was evicting her. On Christmas Eve! On the coldest night of the year!

I called the landlord to see what we could work out. I told him I would come in the day after Christmas and pay her rent if he would promise not to put her and her babies out. He would not budge. I sighed and resigned myself to yet another task before I could go home.

I made out a check and drove the eighteen miles to town to deliver the check and a few items for the children for Christmas. As I handed the land-lord his check, I verbally observed how inconvenient his timing was, how uncaring it appeared to put out this young woman and her children in the cold at Christmas.

"Do you think I don't know what I'm doing?" he replied. "I knew one of you bleeding hearts would come through, simply because of the circum-stances. I just wanted my money."

A LONG WALK

She had already walked three miles when Randy passed her and turned around to pick her up. "Where're you going?" he asked.

"Cookson," she replied, "I have to get to that mission and fill out an application for Christmas."

"I work there. I will take you right to it," he informed her.

When she was finished with the application, she left and began walking home before anyone knew she was gone. When the staff told me about her walking, I grabbed my keys and headed for the truck. I picked her up a mile from the mission and we headed for her house. I didn't know her, she was a new client, so I began by asking where she lived. It was a twelve mile hike one way. I asked what was going on, why she was walking. She said that she and her husband had no car, and everyone they knew to ask wanted gas money to take them anywhere. They simply didn't have any money.

I asked how she was going to keep her appointment at the Christmas Store and how she would get the gifts and food box home. She teared up and began to cry. "I can't stress about that now," she said, "I'll work something out. I prayed for a ride and God gave me one both ways, so I'll have to trust that He will work out something for me."

I was impressed at this woman's faith, even in a discouraging situation, so I pressed her to tell me more about her situation. Her husband was a woodcutter. He was more than willing to work, but someone had stolen his chainsaw six weeks earlier. They had not had any income since.

"I was already getting really tired when that man picked me up, but I knew this was the only way my little girl was going to have anything for Christmas. I told myself, she's only four years old, I'm 31, this may be hard, but I can do it."

A CHRISTMAS STORY

One of the first Christmases that I spent at Cookson brought me to this story. I belonged to the Tahlequah Round-up Club. It was a club of cowboys that put on the rodeos every year in Tahlequah. As Christmas approached they began planning a party for the children of members. I had no children, so l began to look around for some that I could take.

There was a single mother who lived a few miles from the Center and was as poor as anyone I had ever seen. She had two little girls, seven and three. The house that they lived in had no running water, no electricity, and no gas. I would take them food on a regular basis, but she always wanted bologna or other items that she didn't need to cook, she had no way to cook.

Her daughters were very clean and well kept. There was a little stream out behind the house and she took them to the stream every day for a bath...no matter what the weather was like.

I invited them to the party and went shopping. Santa was to be at the party and he needed deliveries specific for the children.

On the night of the party, I took my packages, picked up the girls and drove the eighteen miles to town. The party was typical; games, food, laughing, screaming children, and lots of excitement At long last, Santa arrived and began calling out names. As child after child was called up and given a present, my girls sat strangely quiet. Finally the name of the seven year old was called, she went politely up and sat on the old man's lap. She checked the gift to be sure it had her name on it. Then he called the name of the three year old. She grabbed my leg and would not let go, so I dragged her up, and Santa awarded her the gift. The other children had ripped off the paper and were playing with their toys. I noticed that my seven year old was just holding her gift.

"Aren't you going to open your present and see what Santa Claus brought you," I asked?

"No," she replied, "I think that I will save it so that I have something to open on Christmas."

We do a grave injustice to children when we tell them that they had better watch out, they had better not cry, they had better not pout, Santa Claus is watching, Santa Claus is coming.

Some children are very clear that it doesn't matter how "good" they are, Santa Claus is not coming. This leads some children to conclude that somehow, they are bad.

SAVING FOR CHRISTMAS

The Christmas Store is a vital part of the ministry at Cookson. During the month of November we take applications from families who struggle financially. We collect data on where the family lives, the number of people in the home, whether anyone in the home works, and their income. When the paperwork is finished, each family is given a date and time to come and shop in the Christmas Store.

The Christmas Store is stocked with new gifts for all ages, and parents are allowed to come in a pick out a gift for each child in the family. Children under eight are allowed both a toy and an item of clothing because we don't want parents to have to make a choice of which one is more important. As the parents shop, volunteers are busy collecting socks, underwear, hats mittens, storybooks, coloring books and crayons and stockings full of candy for them. The family also receives a gift; towels, blankets, pillows, sheets, a kitchen item, a calendar, a Christmas ornament, and a sack of toiletries. Each gift is wrapped as it is picked out, and as the family leaves, their cars are loaded with a box of groceries for their Christmas dinner.

One morning, a young, single father came in to shop for his five daughters. His wife had died in November and he lost his hourly job trying to take care of the details that must be attended to after a death. He had no income. He was very selective in his gifts, and gave careful thought to each girl. When he was finished and we had all of his belongings stuffed into big grocery sacks, it came time to settle up. "That will be thirty five cents," I told him.

He pulled out a jar of change and looked me straight in the eye and responded, "Ma'am, I didn't know how I was going to give Christmas to my girls. They lost enough already, what with their mom and all. I been saving since she died and I want you to take all this to pay for my stuff....and thanks! You saved our Christmas."

Later that afternoon I poured out the change and with tears in my eyes I counted $2.10. I prayed under my breath, "Merry Christmas."

CHRISTMAS AGAIN

The last day of the Christmas Store has historically become "Teenage Day." We allow teenage children of the families who qualify, to shop for their families for $1.00 a gift. Teenage Day is a very busy day since some families have up to five teenagers and we only allow one day for shopping.

There were seven shoppers at any given time and ten or more waiting their turn. We moved fast and wrapped fast. As soon as one youth was finished another was herded in. In spite of all the chaos, there was one young man who would not be hurried. He picked out gifts for each member of his family in good time, but when we told him he could pick out something for himself, he shifted into neutral. He wandered around, looking on every table, handling items, and finally just standing. I continued to push others through but I must admit, I was getting irritated. What was he looking for? Was he shoplifting? What was taking him so long?

I kept my eye on him while I rushed around trying to keep the day from becoming complete pandemonium. Finally, it was lunch time and the crowd thinned. I went to him and asked if there was a problem, or a certain item that he was looking for? He ducked his head and wouldn't look me in the eye. Then he asked, "Is it alright if I pick out a baby gift for my new baby instead of myself?"

I looked at his face, trying to see how old he was…fifteen. I told him I didn't know that he had a baby, of course he could pick a gift for her. "And by the way," I said, "pick something for yourself, too."

WORTH SOMETHING

We went to see her and to wish her a Merry Christmas. She will tell you that she is almost 100 years old. She is 95 and expects to live to be a hundred. She will. I have never met anyone so old and yet so spry.

She has no car, so she doesn't get out much. She is energetic and very appreciative. She laughs and teases, the epitome of what I want to be should I ever live so long.

We visited and laughed. As we got ready to leave, she drew my friend up to her and whispered, "Thanks for coming, you made me feel like I was worth something."

You made me feel like I was worth something.

I wonder how many people in the world feel worthless. It is such a simple thing to help people feel like they are worth something. A phone call, a visit, a note, or a gift are small investments to make a person feel like they are worth something.

I remember one of my seminary professors saying one day, if Jesus were to walk into the local grocery store, every person in that store would be touched by Him in some way. I believe that. I believe it is our responsibility to do the same. There should never be a person within our reach who feels worthless. Jesus valued everyone. He gave value to everyone. God calls us to do the same.

PEGGY AND ARNOLD

It is hard for me to believe that anyone in the 20th century still lived the way that Peggy and Arnold lived. They lived in a log cabin with a loft where the children slept. The only heat that they had was wood and they cooked on the wood stove, too. There was no electricity, no running water and no transportation.

I first met them when a dispute erupted on the Tuscarora Reservation over transporting the children to school. The money to transport Tuscarora children was Federal money and was not to be used for Non-Indians. Arnold was a full blood Tuscarora but Peggy was Caucasian. The Tuscarora Tribe is matrilineal, so even though the children were Tuscarora, they were not considered to be Indians. The school refused to drive on to the reservation to pick up non-Indian children. Arnold had tried and tried to convince the school that it was important for his children to go to school, but to no avail. Finally, Arnold walked them to the school bus carrying a shotgun. He made no threats, but it scared the bus driver. Charges were filed and now there was an even bigger problem.

I went to Arnold's house to ask him what I could do. He told me to do whatever I could to assure his children a chance at an education. I went back to my office and called the State Education Department in Albany. In two days, the problem was solved. At least, it was solved for me. I quickly came to realize that once again the bureaucracy had kept a poor man in his place. In spite of his attempts to resolve this issue; his many visits to the school, his appearances at the School Board Meetings, his calls to city officials and Tribal Leaders. He had been unable to solve his problem, but a pastor with a title was able to unravel the red tape in two short days. This was degrading to Arnold and once again affirmed to him that he had no power and was not in charge of his own destiny.

Peggy, Arnold and I became good friends and I went to visit any time that I felt the rigors of ministry were causing me to lose sight of what was important in life. They lived a very simple life and it was easy to regain a sense of appreciation and gratitude in their home. I always took coffee with me, as they rarely had any and this enabled me to leave them with a treat that they seldom afforded themselves.

One day, I walked into their house and there in the middle of the floor was a brand new Kirby Vacuum cleaner. "Peggy?" I asked, "what is this doing here? You don't have a carpet …you don't even have electricity."

"I know," she replied, "I told him that, but he wouldn't listen so I just signed the paper and he left it. Don't worry, he'll be back when I can't pay for it."

"But Peggy," I said, "it will ruin your credit rating." I was truly concerned that this person had been persistent enough to sell her something that she certainly didn't need…indeed, something that she couldn't even use. She was unwilling to compromise her own dignity to convince this salesperson that she was unable to buy this machine.

Peggy looked at me with a strange look on her face. "We ain't got no credit rating. You gotta have money to get a credit rating."

Another assumption! I had entered a conversation with a person from my perspective, from my experience, assuming that my experience would be everyone's experience. It seldom is. I am learning that on the mission field I must be more cognizant of what is around me; to listen with empathetic ears, to see what is not there as well as what is, and above all to preserve the dignity of those persons who have found life to be more of a struggle than a joy.

My last Christmas on the Tuscarora Reservation was one of the best for me. We often believe that it is the poor who have needs and it is our job to fix them. We become the "hero," even "the savior," if I may. We look to the problems of the poor and it is easy to see what is wrong because they are not our problems. We can solve these problems for them. The real revelation comes when we discover that we all have problems, we all have needs, and there are times when the poor can give to us.

There was a man in town who often questioned my work at the Reservation. He wasn't really against it, he simply didn't understand it. He had always believed that poverty was self inflicted and anyone who wanted out could get out simply by getting a job. I tried unsuccessfully to help him understand that it wasn't as easy as that. He was trying to find a quick fix to an old and complicated problem. I explained to him that for Arnold to get a job, he would first have to have a way to find out about a job (he doesn't get a paper.) Then he would have to take a bath in a tub in the front room of his house with water he had heated on the stove. He would have to launder his good clothes the same way and try to get them pressed (it is hard to iron without electricity). He would have to walk six miles to town to fill out an application and if he made it to an interview the response is always, "we'll call you." With no phone and no transportation to and from work, his problems are not solved.

Each time we discussed these issues, Loren would become very thoughtful.

I knew that he was struggling to release some old ideas and to come to grips with the realities of poverty. It was because of this that I invited him to come with me to the Reservation on Christmas Eve to play "Santa." I had several stops to make, but two were especially important.

The first stop was at the home of a woman who came to the mission regularly. We had been there one night preparing for the children's Christmas party. We were wrapping gifts and packing candy sacks and telling stories about when we "found out" about Santa. Bessie's turn finally came around and she said that she had never believed in Santa Claus as a child because her family was extremely poor and Santa never came to their home. I had decided that she needed the opportunity to be surprised by Santa, no matter how old she was.

I rented a Santa suit and we headed out to the reservation. Our first stop was at Bessie's. She opened the door to find our "Santa" standing on her front porch. She had no idea who he was or where he had come from but he had several gifts for her. It was so much fun listening to her tell the story later about how a strange man in a strange car had come to her home and left gifts.

The second stop was at the home of Peggy and Arnold. We stopped down the road so that the children could not see, then we pushed Loren out of the car. There were no lights in the yard, only an oil lamp in the front room. I worried about Loren tripping over something in the yard, but my worries were pointless. He was gone a long time and we began to wonder what was going on.

When he returned to the car he was in tears and couldn't talk. We rode along in silence for a long time and then he said, "I never knew that people lived like that anymore. I went into the house and the children woke up. They were peering over the rail in the loft and I could hear them telling each other that I was Santa Claus. One said, 'see, I told you he was real.' Meri, did you know that they didn't even have a tree? There wasn't a single gift in that house.

"These people don't need me to tell them how to get out of poverty, they don't need me to take care of them, they certainly don't need me to fix everything for them. Who do I think I am? All they need from me is for me to love them and encourage them…but I discovered something else from them tonight, too. That is exactly what I need from them. When I saw the faces of those precious little children peeking out from the loft, their eyes so full of wonder, I knew I wanted to have the opportunity to be around them, to form a bond with them and to glow in the acceptance and love that they can give me. This has been the best Christmas gift you could have ever given me! Thank you."

We must get past the idea that working with the poor is about saving them from their circumstances. When the woman poured the perfume on Jesus and the disciples complained about the expense, Jesus reminded them that the poor would always be with us. The important thing was that the widow felt affirmed…the important thing is that all people feel affirmed. It is important to keep in mind that people, all people, are important because of who they are not because of what they have.

GARDEN ANGEL

Missions are the recipients of many in-kind gifts, especially at Christmas. I was working in the Christmas Store going through the boxes that had been sent earlier in the season. I reached my hand down into a box and pulled out a beautiful garden angel. Now a garden angel is a wonderful gift and one that I would enjoy very much, but I have all of my needs met. Our people are looking for blankets, warm clothing or frying pans. A garden angel is not something that they would choose especially when we were three months from garden season.

I took the angel out of the box and I said, "oh, look! A garden angel. What shall we do with her?"

One of the women had created a display with angel books, candles, and necklaces. She suggested that we put her on that table to draw attention to the other items. As the season went on, we named her Angelica and we began to get silly with her. We would tell her that no one had looked at her today, it didn't look like she was going to get to go home for Christmas this year, but don't worry, we were going to take care of her.

We had been in the Christmas Store for about ten days when the phone rang. It was a social worker from DHS. "Are you doing baskets for Christmas?" she asked.

I explained that we didn't do baskets. We took applications from families in our area and they were allowed to shop at our Christmas Store, a store for low income people. For a token amount, everyone in the family was allowed one gift. In addition, we give every child socks, mittens, hats, color books, crayons, a story book and a stocking full of candy. Every family receives a calendar, a food box with everything they need for Christmas Dinner, and a family gift from us. We also wrap the gifts so the family is ready for Christmas when they leave.

"Do you take referrals?" the social worker inquired.

"Absolutely!" I responded. "What do you need?"

She explained to me that there had been a bad fire in our area a few days before. The two parents were killed in the fire. The two babies were killed in the blaze but the two middle children had survived and were being placed in a grandmother's the home. The grandmother already lived below the poverty level and now, without warning or preparation, she was left with two little mouths to feed. The children came to her without clothes, without shoes, without toothbrushes, all had been burned in the fire. They came without Christmas gifts and it was only five days until Christmas. Was there anything we could do?

We scurried around and found several outfits for the children, shoes, underwear, blankets, towels, hairbrushes, toothbrushes, coats, hats and mittens. The grandmother came in and shopped for gifts, and we loaded her car with everything we could find. As she was finishing up, I told her to pick out something for herself. She acted confused so I explained that it wasn't right for her to sit in her own living room, under her own Christmas tree and have nothing for herself.

"Can I have anything I want?" She questioned.

"Anything you want," I told her.

She went right for that garden angel. We all looked at each other in disbelief. Tears streamed down her face as she carried it up to the table to be wrapped.

"I'll take this," she said. "We don't have a marker for the grave and this looks just like one of the babies that will be spending her Christmas with Jesus this year."

We all sobbed as we wrapped up that little angel destined to mark the grave of two babies buried together at Christmas time. In all of the years that I have served on the mission field, we had never had a garden angel sent to us and we have not had one since but God knew that on this year there was a grandmother that was going to need a marker for her grandbabies grave and He saw to it that some United Methodist somewhere sent one. That is the power of Christmas, God sees the needs of His children and meets them in miraculous ways. God can use even the most simple things to accomplish this for us. This is the miracle of Christmas.

Chapter Nine

"…and you shall be my witnesses
both in Jerusalem, and in all Judea,
and Samaria, and even
to the remotest part of the earth."

Acts 1:8

CONCLUSION

The meeting was almost over. I glanced at my watch to see how long we had been hashing over this new program in the church. Four hours! When I added in the two hour trip each way to attend the meeting, it seemed like a very large investment. It was precious time that would be hard to make up. The time came to vote on the budget for this program and it was reported that the Committee on Finances Administration had rejected the proposed $200,000.00 that we'd requested and only approved $175,000.00. Someone stated that we simply could not begin this ministry with so little money. I was stunned. I was confused. I spoke up, "That is more money than we have to run the entire mission with and we have six buildings and a staff of five."

One of the church leaders leaned over to me and said in a quiet voice, "Well, we pay people what they are worth in the United Methodist Church."

Yes, I think he was kidding, but even if he was, what a statement to be made! What an attitude to be considered. The United States of America is the richest nation the world has ever known and yet it donates less than 2% of its annual income to benevolences, and most of that money is given to libraries, election campaigns, and museums. Less than .05% of that 2% given goes to feed the poor. In layman's terms; one penny out of every one hundred dollars earned in this country is given to the needy.

Money is the one single topic that almost made me ignore the calling that God placed on my life. I didn't want to "beg" for money for the ministry that I was being asked to do. The idea plagued me for weeks. I knew that I wanted to go into mission, but why do missionaries have to find so much of their resources themselves?

I finally decided to seek the counsel of one of my Professors, Dr. W. Dr. W. had served in Afghanistan for many years, in a school for the blind. Now he was at Gordon Conwell Theological Seminary, teaching missions to students who planned to serve.

"Dr. W." I began, "You know that I feel God is directing me to pursue a mission ministry. I am very reluctant to take on a ministry where it is my responsibility to beg for money to help people. There must be another way."

Dr. W. sat quietly for several minutes as he mentally measured the scope of this problem for me and then he simply said to me, "Never be ashamed to ask God's people for God's money to do God's work."

That simple statement has affected my life and ministry for over twenty five years now. God has always used His people to supply every need I have experienced on the mission field, and I believe that He will continue to be our source by utilizing the people of God.

Money is a great servant but a poor master. I believe that God wants us to serve with our time, our talents, our prayers, our contacts, and yes, to Americans most especially…with our money.

EPILOGUE

Three months! Three months! I was given a three month sabbatical to work on this book, and to get some rest. God is so good! I remember last summer I was making lists of all the things that I needed to do, including this book, and I thought to myself, "God, if I only had three months, I could get all of this done." Within six weeks of this thought, the General Board of Global Ministries had decided that missionaries stationed in the same assignment for a long period time should consider a three month sabbatical.

I was so blessed! I had not taken more than two successive weeks of vacation since I had started working as a freshman in high school. Three months! I began to make plans. I bought a calendar with lines for my lists. I made a daily plan so that I would not allow a single minute of the day to be wasted. I began to day dream about leisurely days reading, and writing, and doing what I wanted to do every day. Three months!

I was in for a very frustrating three months. I would plan my day, and someone would call and need something from me. I would plan my day and something else would come up. I would make my plans and something would go wrong. In the three months that I was off, I made twenty four trips to a doctor's office, sat through four surgeries, took care of children on four different weekends, dealt with three deaths, and pastored the church through Palm Sunday and Easter.

I remember one specific night. I told a friend that I was *not* going anywhere the next day. I was *not* going to answer the phone. I was *not* answering the door. I was going to sleep late, take a long hot bath, read, relax and have one day for myself. My exact words to my friend were, "short of somebody dying, I am going to have *one* day for me."

The phone rang at 5:30 am. I stumbled out of bed, begrudging the fact that the phone had interfered with my day to sleep in. "Short of somebody dying" rang in my thoughts as the person at the other end of the line told me a family member had been killed in a car wreck a few hours earlier and they needed someone to watch their children while the family gathered and made plans for a funeral.

I began to get depressed. My prayer life in the morning was weighted with the question, "Why?" "Why can't I seem to have any time?" "Why can't I do what I want to do?" "Why doesn't anything ever work out the way I planned?"

The last week of the sabbatical, as I was working and lamenting the fact that my three months was almost over and I had not accomplished anywhere near the volume of work that I had planned, I remembered a story. It seems a man acquired a new hunting dog and he was anxious to show it off. He called a hunting buddy and asked him to go hunting. It was a beautiful day and the lake was quiet as they sat in the boat together. Suddenly a duck flew up out of the water and over the boat. The owner of the dog raised his rifle and fired, "Bang! Bang!" The duck fell into the water and the man turned to his dog and said, "Go get the duck."

The dog jumped out of the boat, ran across the water, grabbed the duck, ran back across the water, and climbed into the boat. The owner proudly looked at his dog and waited for a response from his friend. None came. They sat very quietly for a while, and suddenly another duck flew out of the water and over the boat. This time the man's friend raised his rifle, "Bang! Bang!" The duck fell into the water.

The owner of the dog said, "Go get the duck." The dog jumped out of the boat, ran across the water, picked up the duck, ran back across the water, and climbed back into the boat. The owner of the dog was certain that this time his friend would at least comment on the dog's skills, but no comment came.

They sat there for a while longer when suddenly a duck flew out of the water, over the boat. The man raised his rifle, "Bang! Bang!" The duck fell into the lake. "Go get the duck" the man said with a little less enthusiasm. The dog jumped out of the boat, ran across the water, picked up the duck, ran back across the water, and climbed back into the boat.

This time the man just couldn't stand it anymore. "You notice anything about my dog?" the man asked.

"I been studying on that for a while." his friend replied. He was quiet for a few minutes and then he said, "That dog don't know how to swim, does he?"

The friend was obviously focusing on the wrong thing and missed the point entirely.

"Focused on the wrong thing and missed the point entirely." This little voice kept repeating that over and over in my mind. "You were focused on the wrong thing and missed the point, entirely."

So what was the point of three months of frustration? I didn't want to miss the point. I believe that the point was this: whether or not I go into an office, mission work does *not* take a sabbatical. Mission work, and the need for mission work, does not take a rest. The more I became focused on me and what I wanted out of the sabbatical, the more frustrated I became. I was focused on the wrong thing.

We need to take time for ourselves, that is a fact. But when we become so consumed with our time, our schedules, or our tasks, that we lose sight of people and the needs around us, then we have become focused on the wrong thing. We are missing the point entirely. God gives us a heart for others, that is something that is difficult to take a sabbatical from. Rest? Yes. But not at the expense of need.